Automotive Fire Analysis

An Engineering Approach

Gregor   CVFI

L&J ® **Lawyers & Judges Publishing Company, Inc.**
Tucson, Arizona

This publication is designed to provide accurate and authoritative information in regard to the subject matter covered. It is sold with the understanding that the publisher is not engaged in rendering legal, accounting, or other professional service. If legal advice or other expert assistance is required, the services of a competent professional person should be sought.

—From a Declaration of Principles jointly adopted by
a Committee of the American Bar Association
and a Committee of Publishers and Associations.

The publisher, editors and authors must disclaim any liability, in whole or in part, arising from the information in this volume. The reader is urged to verify the reference material prior to any detrimental reliance thereupon. Since this material deals with legal, medical and engineering information, the reader is urged to consult with an appropriate licensed professional prior to taking any action that might involve any interpretation or application of information within the realm of a licensed professional practice.

 **Lawyers & Judges
Publishing Company, Inc.**

P.O. Box 30040 • Tucson, AZ 85751-0040
(800) 209-7109 • FAX (800) 330-8795
e-mail: sales@lawyersandjudges.com
www.lawyersandjudges.com

Barnett, Gregory J.
  Automotive fire analysis : an engineering approach / Gregory J. Barnett, AE, ASE, CFEI, CVFI. -- Third edition.
    pages cm
  Includes bibliographical references and index.
  ISBN 978-1-936360-15-4 (softcover : alk. paper) -- ISBN 1-936360-15-2 (softcover : alk. paper)
  1. Automobiles--Fires and fire prevention. 2. Fire investigation. I. Title.
  TL241.B37 2013
  629.2'31--dc23
                                          2013003340
ISBN 13: 978-1-936360-15-4
ISBN 10: 1-936360-15-2
Printed in the United States of America
10 9 8 7 6 5 4 3 2 1

Contents

Introduction

This latest edition contains the most updated information available on vehicle fire analysis. The biggest addition is in the second training DVD. This addresses the misunderstandings and misconceptions of DC electrical fire. The DVD contains unique photographs depicting what to seek out in DC electrical fires. Additionally, it addresses the "copper argument" on what the CFI and investigating engineer should look for in DC electrical fires to determine if the damage to the wiring is from an electrical source or from heat impingement. Also included are discussion on battery types, alternator failure leading to fire, and the standard of care required by automotive industry standards for repair work performed.

There are expanded sections covering hybrid vehicles, lithium-ion battery construction, how Supplemental Restraint Systems operate, failure modes, and how the memory being built into crash data recorder systems can be used to assist fire investigation.

Other added sections cover the topics of gas and electric golf cart fire, and how Power Distribution Modules operate. Unique subjects such as PAG oil fires, a discussion of refrigerant types, and a discussion of the new flammable R-1234yf refrigerant system are also included.

This book will make an excellent addition to any fire investigator or engineer's library.

Chapter 1

Introduction

1.1 Background of the Problem

Automobile fire is a concern not only to the owner of the vehicle, but also to the manufacturer and the insurance carrier for the owner of the vehicle. Fire is of paramount concern from both a safety aspect and a financial aspect. For example, in a hypothetical situation a vehicle catches fire shortly after the owner has parked it in his home garage. The fire spreads and the home becomes engulfed in the ensuing blaze. The owner is now out of a place to live and his automobile is destroyed. The two most expensive purchases (typically) in a person's life have been damaged beyond use in one short span of time. If our hypothetical person works from a home office, the claim could include business interruption. Beyond claims for simple property damages, there also may be bodily injury or even death considerations.

Who is responsible? What if the automobile is out of warranty by quite a significant margin? Is the automobile manufacturer responsible for just the vehicle or the house too? Is the manufacturer responsible at all? What about automobile safety standards? Didn't the engineers foresee this safety defect? Was there a defective design? These are all good questions. However, as with most legal issues, the answers may not be quite so simple. The issues become complex due to: non-stock modifications to the engine and powertrain, non-OEM equipment added such as stereo systems or power inverters, lack of absolute determination of design defect from the fire debris, and others which will be discussed in later chapters.

A confounding factor is that an automobile is legally defined in all 50 states as "chattel." This means that this type of personal property is movable and transferable. An automobile can cross state boundaries with relative ease. It can even be licensed in one state and operated in other states. Thus, an automobile is quagmired in both federal and varying states' legal codes. For example, California requires that smog equipment have a seven-year/70,000-mile warranty whereas federal regulations require only a five-year/50,000-mile warranty. If the vehicle caught fire at 60,000 miles due to a defect in the smog system, the case would be much stronger if the loss occurred in a "California car."

There is a legal process called "subrogation." It is specifically for recovering damages incurred by a first party against a liable third party. However, this process is subjected to the same obfuscation by state code. This topic will be addressed fully in the text. The nuances of subrogation issues are of particular importance to the investigating engineer so that proper groundwork can be laid to support the claim.

1.2 Reasons for Lack of Information on Vehicle Fire

Cost is one of the principal difficulties for the establishment of proper scientific testing or study in the area of automobile operational fire. All vehicle fires have the propensity for being a unique event. The cost to set ten of the same make and model vehicles on fire merely to study the fire characteristics would be astronomical. Given that there are approximately 3,000 different vehicle trim levels for the different models sold in the North American Market at any given time, it immediately becomes patently cost prohibitive to test all vehicles.

An ancillary consideration is the mindset of any given manufacturer in the arena of marketing and publicity. This author has yet to encounter in 35 years of experience in the automobile industry any manufacturer who does not mind if the word got out that their products had a propensity for catching fire. Obviously, any warranty repairs for vehicle fire will be kept a closely guarded secret. Even legally required disclosure to NHTSA is done reluctantly by the manufacturer. A common legal defense here is to settle all fire claims by requiring all claimants to sign a "no publicity or public statements" release before the settlement funds are released. If this type of publicity were to get out to the general public, obviously it would have a devastating effect on sales of that product.

1.3 Statement of the Problem

The problem can be quite simply stated that there exists only modest research material in the form of published scientific research papers, books, or other types of validated studies on the subject of automobile fire diagnosis. The vast majority of vehicle fire study is in the area of post-collision burn deaths of trapped passengers. As noted above, even if a manufacturer conducts a study on the subject, the data will be kept internal particularly if the results indicate marginal compliance with regulations. Thus, the availability of information to inquiring engineers is quite limited.

The Society of Automotive Engineers does not have a published standard for informational purposes or as a guide for anything on the subject of automotive fire behavior. The SAE does not have a guide for recognizing arson or other incendiary factors. Most engineers do not receive any training as an arson investigator.

The next group that has an interest in automotive fire are arson investigators and certified fire investigators. However, the biggest problem areas here are that automobile fire studies or statistics are skewed when they are gathered by these groups because they do not receive any automotive engineering training as part of their normal course of study.

Typically, the only time a fire investigator or a fire department even sees an automobile fire is when the blaze has become a "large order" (i.e., big blazing) fire and their services are required to extinguish the blaze. For example, a fuel line has ruptured onto the hot exhaust and caught fire.

The vast majority of automobile fires are "small order" (i.e., smoldering low flames) fires, not "large order." The vehicle will malfunction, a small flare-up or copious amounts of smoke appear, then the fire simply snuffs itself out due to lack of fuel or ignition mechanism. The vehicle is then towed to a repair shop to be repaired. The fire department isn't even called out. Thus, the only type of automobile fires a fireman or fire investigator sees are arson-based fires or accidental fires of "large order." This leads the investigator to believe that all automobile fires are "large order" fires and, in turn, will skew the statistics kept by the fire departments and state fire marshal's office. Fire department personnel and arson investigation associations will have a complete lack of experience in the quantity and size of typical automobile fires. Further, as noted above, fire department personnel and certified fire investigators are not trained in automotive technology, automotive codes and standards, or material engineering as part of their firefighting or fire investigator training.

Obviously, both the investigating engineer and the certified fire investigator both desire to arrive at a successful analysis after a vehicle has caught fire. It is important that the primary failed part be identified so that a subrogation action can be undertaken with confidence and the manufacturer or insurance carrier can advise its legal staff.

The initial research conducted by this author reveals that only modest amounts of research have been conducted in this area. The most germane SAE research paper located thus far is dated 1981. This hardly qualifies as a recent study even under the most lax definition of the scientific method. By contrast, there were 192 SAE research papers located on post-collision fire analysis and design safety issues. As noted above, there is some research material available, but nothing resembling a comprehensive guide for critical analysis on an engineering level.

1.4 Purpose of the Book

The purpose of this book is to produce a critical analysis guide for analyzing operational mode automotive fire which compiles and analyzes the research undertaken to date by manufacturers, standards organizations and private institutions. Additionally, the book will introduce data accumulated on automobile fire science research conducted by this author.

Ideally, the research will answer the question of why the interpretation of fire debris from operational mode failure analysis varies so drastically. It will provide a comprehensive view into understanding the mechanisms for automobile fire, BTU and fire load analysis, primary failed part analysis with confidence, and recognition of arson indicators.

This book is designed for intermediate and advanced personnel whether that person is a certified fire investigator or engineer. It is a compilation of automotive information not found in any one publication. It goes much further into depth than the approximately 20 pages the NFPA 921 guide offers on automotive fire. However, it is not a step-by-step methodology to arrive at the primary failed part. Any expert opinion expressed should be based upon as much fact as can be garnered from the available evidence.

1.5 Definitions of Terms

To maintain consistency with California Civil Code, this author makes no statement nor proffers any information which may or should be construed as legal advice. Typically, any legal advice or legal services provided within a given state must be performed by a licensed attorney of that state. Any legal definitions of terms will be paraphrased from legal dictionaries. These definitions may not be similar or accurate in all 50 states. This author directs the reader to legal counsel for further clarification of any legal questions.

The reason that the NFPA 921 guide was chosen for definition of terms almost exclusively is that the National Fire Protection Association is one of the most influential trade associations in the U.S. The vast majority of states' fire marshals' offices or local fire authorities will adopt the NFPA Standards and National Codes in part or virtually verbatim into state or local building codes. The NFPA has written and established the National Building Code, the National Electrical Code, and the National Fire Protection Equipment Code, along with others. The definitions found in the NFPA 921 guide are quite accurate and generally accepted by professional firemen and engineers throughout the U.S.

The NFPA has requested that the following paragraph be listed with the use of their copyright material:

> Reprinted with permission from NFPA 921-2011, Guide for Fire and Explosion Investigation, Copyright © 2001, National Fire Protection Association, Quincy, MA 02269. This reprinted material is not the complete and official position of the NFPA on the referenced subject, which is represented only by the standard in its entirety.

Not all of the definitions are sourced exclusively from the NFPA 921 guide because some terms are much more closely associated with Society of Automotive Engineers and Automotive Industry accepted definitions.

None of the definitions places the burned vehicle in a structure. These definitions and all of the information contained in this book deal with a vehicle burning by itself outside a structure. The focus is to analyze the product system failure that led to a fire. If a vehicle is inside a burning structure, the entire contents and the vehicle structure will be exposed to transfer temperatures abnormal to a system failure while the vehicle was running or parked. If the vehicle were parked inside a structure and was the cause of the fire that spread to the structure from the vehicle, then distinctly different burn patterns will be present compared to accidental fire for vehicles parked outside a structure.

accelerant. An agent, often an ignitable liquid, used to initiate a fire or increase the rate of growth or spread of a fire.[27]

accident. An unplanned event that interrupts an activity and sometimes causes injury or damage. A chance occurrence arising from unknown causes; an unexpected happening due to carelessness, ignorance, and the like.[27]

ambient. The localized conditions or surroundings of an event such as an open flame. As used in this thesis, the ambient temperature is the temperature of the air immediately surrounding a fire.[27]

ampacity. The current, in amperes (A), that a conductor can carry continuously under the conditions of use without exceeding its temperature rating.[27]

ampere. The unit of electric current that is equivalent to a flow of one coulomb per second. One coulomb is defined as $6.24 \times 1,018$ electrons.[27]

arc. A high-temperature luminous electric discharge between a polarity or induction gap; an electrical spark which can range from a small spark to wire-melting capacity.[27]

arc beading. The propensity of a copper wire to create a small bead-like drip or rounded collection of molten material at the point of separation when an electrical circuit is overloaded. Generally accompanied by heat discoloration.[27]

area of origin. Portion of automobile where fire started. May not necessarily be area of greatest heat signs.[27]

arson. The crime of maliciously and intentionally, or recklessly, starting a fire or causing an explosion.[27]

autoignition or **autoignition temperature**. (1) The surface temperature experienced by the potential fuel load which is absorbing radiant or convective heat, or is electrically creating its own heat, to the point of separation of the volatile organic compounds which self-ignite when subjected to sufficient heat and oxygen. Also see **stochiometric ratio.** (2) The state of creating a flame from smoke by exposing flammable liquid or solid to a non-piloted (no spark or open flame) ignition heat source.[27,17]

battery. Device used to store direct current electricity. Automotive battery for the purpose of this study has a stated capacity to be 675 cold cranking amps.[17]

BLEVE. Acronym for "boiling liquid expanding vapor explosion." In automotive application, this is referred to as the explosion of the fuel tank when the fuel tank is being exposed to other flames or heat source.[27]

British thermal unit (BTU). The quantity of heat required to raise the temperature of 1 pound of water 1°F at the pressure of one atmosphere and ambient air temperature of 60°F. A British thermal unit is equal to 1,055 joules, 1.055 kilojoules, and 252.15 calories. Ten to the exponent of 4 equals one therm.[28]

calorie. The amount of heat necessary to raise 1 gram of water 1°C at 15°C ambient air temperature. There are 252.15 Calories per BTU.[27]

calorimeter. Instrument used to determine the potential BTU load of a given test piece by burning the piece then measuring the presence of flammable hydrocarbons and volatile organic compounds.[29]

carrier. Refers to a company that sells insurance in the U.S. market as used in this text.

code. (1) A standard that is an extensive compilation of provisions covering broad subject matter or that is suitable for adoption into law independently of other codes and standards. (2) A body of law for either state or federal application (e.g., the Civil Code of California or the Federal Code of Regulations).[3]

combustible. Capable of burning, generally, in air under normal conditions of ambient temperature and pressure, unless otherwise specified. Combustion can occur in cases where an oxidizer other than the oxygen in the air is present. Combustion temperatures can increase dramatically when the combustion process is subjected to contained heat and pressure.[27]

combustible gas indicator ("sniffer"). An instrument that samples air and indicates whether or not there are combustible vapors present. Typically used as a field instrument when arson is suspected.[27]

conduction. Heat transfer to another body or within a body by direct contact; heat transfer to another body via exposure of both the heat source and the transfer body to same contact area. For example, flames on one side of a metal firewall cause the firewall to heat. This in turn will cause the plastic touching on the other side of the firewall to catch fire.[27]

convection. Heat transfer by circulation within a medium such as a gas or liquid; heat transfer to another body via exposure to super-heated air.[27]

current. The element in both AC and DC electricity which provides the electromotive force. Also see **ampere**. This is the part of the electrical flow which is the power (i.e., voltage will cause the electricity to flow down the wire). Without amperage, voltage by itself will not cause the motor to spin its armature or to light a lamp. Amperage combined with voltage will cause the motor to spin its armature or light a lamp.[12]

drop down. The spread of fire by the dropping or falling of burning materials. Synonymous with "fall down" fire.[27]

extinguish. To cause to cease burning.[27]

failure. Distortion, breakage, deterioration, or other fault in an item, component, system, assembly, or structure that results in unsatisfactory performance of the function for which it was designed.[3]

failure analysis. A logical, systematic examination of an item, component, assembly, or structure and its place and function within a system, conducted in order to identify and analyze the probability, causes, and consequences of potential and real failures.[27]

fire. A rapid oxidation process with the evolution of light and heat in varying intensities. Also considered the eruption of open flames not intended by normal operation of the automobile.[27]

fire analysis. The process of determining the origin, cause, development, and responsibility as well as the failure analysis of a fire or explosion.[27]

fire dynamics. The detailed study of how chemistry, fire science, and the engineering disciplines of fluid mechanics and heat transfer interact to influence fire behavior.[27]

fire investigation. The process of determining the origin, cause, and development of a fire or explosion.[27]

FMVSS 302. Acronym standing for Federal Motor Vehicle Safety Standard. Refers to the Federal Code of Regulations, Title 49, Chapter 5, Section 571,

Subsection 302. This is the federal standard which defines the minimum flammability standards of the interior components in a vehicle for sale in the U.S. market.

fire science. The body of knowledge concerning the study of fire and related subjects such as combustion, flame, products of combustion, heat release, heat transfer, fire and explosion chemistry, fire and explosion dynamics, thermodynamics, kinetics, fluid mechanics, fire safety and their interaction with people, structures, and the environment. For the purposes of this study the definition is restricted to automotive applications.[27]

flame front. The leading edge of burning gasses of a combustion reaction.[27]

flammable limits. The upper or lower concentration limits at a specified temperature and pressure of a flammable gas or a vapor. This is expressed as a percentage of flammable gas or vapor in relation to oxygen content.[27] Also see **stochiometric ratio**.

flammable range. Concentration range of a flammable gas or a vapor of a flammable liquid in air that can be ignited.[27] For example, given materials cannot burn above or below a stated range of heat characteristic of the flammability of those materials. Burning paper will not create a temperature of 6,000°F.

flashover. (1) A transition phase in the development of a contained fire in which surfaces exposed to thermal radiation reach ignition temperature more or less simultaneously and fire spreads rapidly throughout the space. (2) The point in a fire's development where the volatile organic compound content in the smoke preceding the flame front becomes hot enough and concentrated enough to burn across its face spreading the burn. Sometimes referred to as "flammable carbon monoxide."[27]

fuel load. The total quantity of combustible contents of a building, space, or fire area, including interior trim. The sum total of burnable material localized to the area of ignition.[27]

gasoline. Fuel which propels most automobiles. Will exhibit BTU load release characteristics of approximately 115,000–160,000 BTU/minute. Not flammable in liquid state. Vaporous state is highly flammable and explosive.[32]

glowing combustion. Luminous burning of solid material without a visible flame. Also see **pyrolysis**.[27]

heat. A form of energy characterized by vibration of molecules and capable of initiating and supporting chemical changes and changes of state.[27]

heat flux. The measure of the rate of heat transfer to a surface expressed in kilowatts per minute squared, BTU's per minute squared, or kilojoules per minute squared.[27]

heat release rate (HRR). The rate at which heat energy is generated by burning or combustion processes.[27]

high order fire. The presence of a high positive pressure combined with the sudden release and ignition of a flammable liquid or highly flammable solid. Causes immediate and higher spread rate of open flames along with greater consumption of localized flammable materials. A high order fire indicates the presence of an accelerant in the burn area.[27]

incendiary. A fire where there are indicators that a flammable liquid or other accelerant was present and that the cause of the fire is deliberate.[27]

ignition. The process of initiating self-sustained combustion. In automobiles this refers to the spark provided by the ignition coil to ignite the gasoline in the combustion chamber.[17]

spontaneous ignition. Initiation of combustion of a material by an internal chemical or biological reaction that has produced sufficient heat to ignite the material.[27]

joule. The preferred SI unit of heat, energy or work; there are 4.184 joules in a calorie, and 1,055 joules in a British thermal unit. A watt is 1 joule per second. Generally used as a unit of measurement of higher quantities of electrical energy.[27]

kilowatt. One thousand watts. Preferred unit of measurement for heat, energy or work for mechanical energy and electrical energy.

liquid—combustible or **flammable**. A liquid having a flash point at or above 100°F (37.8°C). A flammable liquid is distinguished from a combustible liquid by definition of having a flash point below 100°F and having a vapor pressure not exceeding 40 psia at the same temperature.[27]

flash point of a liquid. The lowest temperature of a liquid, as determined by specific laboratory tests, at which the liquid gives off vapors at a sufficient rate to support a momentary flame across its surface.[27]

HVAC or HeVAC. Acronym which stands for heating, ventilation, and air conditioning. Also referred to as the "air suitcase" on an automobile. This is the ducting system on an automobile located either under the dashboard, on the engine side of the firewall, or both, which houses the heater core, air conditioning evaporator, and ventilation fan. Some modern vehicles will be equipped with heater and air conditioning for the rear seats. The "rear air" systems will have independent controls than the front (dashboard) air system.[17]

loom. Wiring loom on an automobile. Refers to the bundled wiring. May be bundled with black vinyl electrical tape, convolute conduit (crinkle tube), or both.

low order fire. Open flames which are characterized by moderate rise in localized positive pressure to the area of ignition. Consumption of localized flammable materials will be consistent with the flammability of such materials. A low order fire does not indicate the presence of an accelerant.[27]

nanocomposite. Refers to any one of a variety of polymeric compounds where the plastic is bonded with inert materials. This has the effect of creating a blend of plastic material which has the visible appearance of its more flammable cousins but will not ignite or burn unless an accelerant or other form of piloted heat is present.

noncombustible material. A material that, in the form in which it is used and under the condition anticipated, will not ignite, burn, support combustion, or release flammable vapors when subjected to fire or heat.[27]

ohm. Unit of measurement for the resistance to electrical flow between two points in an electrical circuit.[12]

Ohm's law. A simple formula used to express the relationship between voltage, current and resistance in an electrical circuit.[12]

overload. Refers to the continued operation of electrical equipment beyond or in excess of normal, full-load rating of ampacity of the wire or equipment. Overload in a circuit will cause it to heat up.[12]

plastic. (1) Any of a wide range of natural or synthetic organic materials of high molecular weight that can be formed by pressure, heat, extrusion, and other methods into desired shapes. (2) The property in ferrous metals where the molecular structure has become weakened by the exposure to oligocyclic stress but has not yet bent or passed the yield point.[27,28]

polymeric. Substance formed by linking together molecules of similar or different monomers to form substances of high molecular weight and differing characteristics.[17]

pour point. (1) Of a fuel oil, nominally the temperature 3°C above which the fuel will just flow under its own weight. A measure of the low-temperature flow characteristics of a fuel. (2) Of a lubricant, a test for the gelling tendency of paraffinic oils at low temperatures.[17]

pyrolysis. The chemical decomposition of a compound into one or more substances by heat alone. The distilling of carbon from any number of substances into a more flammable state. Generally requires exposure to low heat for extended periods of time before pyrolytic carbon to form.[27]

scientific method. The systematic pursuit of knowledge involving the recognition and formulation of a problem, the collection of data through observation and experiment, and the formulation and testing of a hypothesis.[27]

spalling. The pitting or chipping which occurs to concrete or masonry surfaces.[27] Spalling will also occur when concrete is exposed to high heat such as flaming gasoline from a ruptured gas tank. Spalling can will also be found occurring accidentally as a course of business at welding and blacksmith shops.

stochiometric ratio. Refers to the rate of burn ability. When the flaming or exploding mixture of gasses reach a ratio of 14.7.1, then optimum conditions for burning or exploding are achieved. This means when the area immediately surrounding the burn or explosion contains 14.7 parts of oxygen to one part of fuel, then optimal consumption of gasses occurs.[35]

thermal inertia. Refers to the property of combustible materials to trap heat and, thereby, increase heat transfer potential into other non-flaming materials. This will have the effect of increasing temperatures achieved within a flaming structure greater than the sum of the individual load potentials.[27]

thermoplastic. Plastic materials which are characterized by softening, melting, and dripping when exposed to (relatively) low temperatures.[27]

thermoset plastic. Plastic materials that are hardened into a permanent shape in the manufacturing process and will not soften, drip, or melt when subjected to heat.[27]

transfer temperature. Refers to the ability to communicate heat within a flaming structure. In automobile fire the interior materials and engine compartment materials will have extremely low transfer temperature characteristics unless a flammable hydrocarbon or liquid catches fire. For example, a smoldering piece of upholstery will not transfer heat to surrounding surfaces like burning gasoline will.

1.6 Limitations of the Book

This book is limited primarily by cost factors. Obviously, it is not financially feasible to set every make and model of automobile on fire to make a study of the fire behavior as the vehicle burns. A second limitation is that safety codes for automobile manufacturing vary from country to country. What may be legal to produce and operate on the highway in one country is not in another. This book is limited to the requirements for vehicle sale in the U.S. market. A third limitation is that when a research organization or foundation is presented with the option of studying property damage or personal injury, then the personal injury will win the research dollars every time. As noted above, there is far more research performed on automobile fire in the post-collision emollition of passengers than in the normal operational mode. Therefore, the critical analysis path will produce a guide which will be based, at least in part, on anecdotal evidence and research conducted by this author.

Another factor to consider is that vehicle fire is defined as a chaotic event. Chaos does not model well mathematically. The confounding factors cannot be calculated with any degree of certainty. As with the fire science of buildings, fire displays only a propensity for similar behavior. There is not enough of any single fire type so that proper statistical analysis methods can be employed. The chaos of the accidental fire event on an automobile will not lend itself to simple trend forecasting.

For example, in any given production run there will not be 100-percent failure of any given part. Even if a part shows a propensity to fail and to catch fire, there will not be 100 percent of the failed parts catching fire. It is simply not possible to accurately predict the moment in time when a given failure will occur or the percentage of part failures which result in a fire. Simply stated, empirical study of this topic will not work and is not the appropriate method for study on this subject.

Thus, the only education by which information can be successfully accrued is through critical analysis of the available information, understanding of the application of the codes and standards, and studying automobile fire through anecdotal-type information.

Chapter 2

History of Codes and Standards

2.1 Introduction

In the early days of automobiles, safety was virtually unheard of. For example, until the late 1940s automobiles used plate glass in the windshield and side glass. Seatbelts didn't become required equipment until 1968. Safety was a pretty hard sell to management and design engineers.

From a manufacturer's point of view, the main objective was and still is to make and sell as many automobiles as possible at the lowest possible cost. If an engineer happened on an idea which could save the manufacturer ten cents on the production of any given vehicle line, he or she would likely get a bonus and paid vacation that year. New ideas which proposed that the manufacturer would have to outlay profits in the name of safety had to demonstrate that the consumer would be willing to spend the extra money for that safety improvement. If the consumer didn't perceive the safety improvement as a positive reason to spend more, then the idea was virtually doomed.

Two famous examples of early safety production concerns are Volvo and Ford. Volvo developed the three-point safety belt in 1953. It did not become available as standard equipment until 1959. Ford offered the Edsel model as being one of the safest vehicles on the road. The poor sales of this model are legendary. Vehicle safety was proving to be difficult to sell to consumers in the 1950s and most of the 1960s.

In 1966 the National Highway Traffic and Safety Administration (NHTSA) was formed by the signing of the National Traffic and Motor Vehicle Safety Act (15 U.S.C. § 1391). This new code expanded the Highway Safety Act of 1964 (23 U.S.C. § 402). With the stroke of a presidential pen, a new era of safety was ushered in.

The National Traffic and Motor Vehicle Safety Act established the authority of NHTSA to regulate the safety of vehicles sold in the U.S. market. The burden of making our automobiles and highways safer was clearly their manifesto. NHTSA was granted the authority to perform safety testing and to administer safety codes. These safety codes are commonly known as Federal Motor Vehicle Safety Standards (FMVSS). The older United States Code sections defining highway safety were superceded. The formal designation for transportation codes regarding vehicles with a gross weight rating of less than 10,000 pounds (most cars and light trucks) is the Federal Code of Regulations, Title 49, Chapter 5, Section 571.

The first order of business for NHTSA was to order seatbelts to be standard equipment on every vehicle sold in the U.S. market. Within ten months, dozens of other safety standards were adopted from lamp specifications to tire performance. Flammability standards were not far behind. On December 2, 1971 FMVSS Number 302—Interior Flammability went into effect.

Before going into the requirements of the code, the point must be stressed that there is a good deal of difference between a code and a standard. For example, in order to sell a vehicle in the U.S. market the manufacturer is required to comply with the FMVSS regulations that apply to the type of vehicle it is selling. These FMVSS codes are considered the bare minimum standards by which a vehicle can be sold in the U.S. market.

There are several "standards" organizations such as the Society of Automotive Engineers (SAE), the International Standards Organization (ISO), the American National Standards Institute (ANSI), and many others who form committees to study and establish industry standards. Many times these safety standards will be superior to the FMVSS standards. However, these standards are "recommended practices," not legally required codes. If a manufacturer chooses to produce a vehicle in accordance with an industry-recommended practice that is superior to—and generally more costly than—the equivalent FMVSS code, then such practice is allowed. The only prohibition is that the manufacturer cannot produce a vehicle which is below the FMVSS code. The main point here is that a Federal Motor Vehicle Safety Standard, although called a "standard," is actually a federal law. However, a safety standard from a standards organization is not.

2.2 Federal Motor Vehicle Safety Standard Number 302: Interior Flammability

From a practical perspective, a motor vehicle is little more than a speeding gas can with a sofa mounted on it. Given the array of options available on most vehicles, the mechanisms for operational failure and resultant fire are numerous. Early motor vehicles used cotton batting, mohair, and natural fibers to upholster and insulate the vehicle interior. These early vehicles would smolder, ignite, and sustain a flame quite well. Much like the upholstered chairs or sofas found in the home, something as simple as an errantly discarded cigarette would ignite the material into a giant blazing inferno.

Federal Code of Regulations, Title 49, Chapter 5, Section 571, Subsection 302 (FMVSS 302) became the flammability resistance standard. The intent of FMVSS 302 was to make the materials which comprise the interior of a vehicle resistant to cigarettes and matches. This standard established the minimum burn resistance standards for selling a vehicle in the U.S. market. The standard applies to all passenger cars, multipurpose passenger vehicles, trucks, and buses with a gross weight rating of less than 10,000 pounds.

The components which specifically must comply to the standard are as follows:

- seat cushions
- seat backs
- seat belts
- headlining
- convertible tops
- arm rests
- all trim panels including door, front, rear, and side panels
- compartment shelves
- head restraints
- floor coverings
- sun visors
- curtains
- wheelhouse coverings
- engine compartment covers
- mattress covers, and

- any other interior materials including padding and crash deployed elements that are designed to absorb energy on contact by occupants in the event of a crash.

Section 4.2 of the FMVSS 302 code also requires that "any portion of a single or composite material which is within 13 mm (approximately 0.5") of the occupant compartment air space shall meet the requirements of Section 4.3."

The most important section of FMVSS 302 is Section 4.3. Section 4.3(a) requires that all of the material components mentioned above shall not burn, nor transmit a flame front across its surface, at a rate of more than 102 mm per minute.

This is important because it establishes a burn resistance timeline. This is a significant tool for the engineer to use to validate a fire as accidental or to conclude that the fire was incendiary.

Sections 5.1.1 through 5.2.3 describe the proper testing required, the test oven to be used in testing, the preparation of material samples to be tested, and most importantly the formula required for burn time calculation. That formula is:

$$B = 60 \times (D/T)$$

in which

B = burn rate in millimeters per minute,
D = length the flame travels in millimeters, and
T = time in seconds for the flame to travel D millimeters.

If the specimen being tested snuffs itself out before burning its full length, then that material is deemed to be in compliance with the code.[13]

For example, if the minimum requirement of a seat burning at a rate of no greater than 102 mm per minute (about 4.5 inches) is divided into the average length of a bench seat of 53–55 inches there should be a burn time of 11–15 minutes for a vehicle fire to consume most of one bench seat. This presumes that the seat foam is of a type which will support flaming combustion. If the engineer is reading a fire department report which establishes a very short response time, such as 6–10 minutes along with an extinguishment time of 1 minute, then a fairly small portion of the vehicle's interior should be burned with some smoke damage and some minor radiant heat damage. If the fire has consumed a greater portion of the available interior materials in a short period of time, the engineer will have to answer "how" in addition to "why" this material was destroyed in a manner inconsistent with FMVSS 302. As was noted in the introduction, most operational mode vehicle fires are low order in nature.

There are some significant factors to address here. FMVSS 302 does not require the same burn resistance of components inside the dashboard such as the instrumentation cluster, the wiring, electric motors, solenoids, vacuum activators, switches, or the heater or air conditioner ducting (HVAC). These components can and do support flame quite well. In fact, most wiring on modern vehicles does not have anything more fire resistant than ordinary polyvinyl chloride (PVC) or polyethylene (PE) insulation. High temperature coatings such as "THHN" ratings are not equipped on motor vehicles. These fire mechanisms will be covered more in depth in the text. The important point is that FMVSS 302 does not apply to every single component in the interior air space.

2.3 Society of Automotive Engineers Standard J369

This standard was originally issued by the SAE in March 1969. This is the standard on which FMVSS 302 was originally modeled. Unfortunately, as is true with most of the FMVSS standards, FMVSS 302 has fallen drastically behind the innovations in the world of polymerics and composite plastics.

SAE J369 was studied in committee again in the late 1970s. The standard was reissued in updated format in June 1989 and once again in January 1994. As innovations in plastics expanded the use of less and less flammable formulas, the SAE J369 standard attempted to keep abreast of the changes. Notably, it has been ten years since the last form of the standard was reissued. Numerous advances have been made in the meantime.

However, FMVSS 302 was last reviewed for changes and updates in 1971, when it went into effect. Even though the flammability resistance standard for FMVSS 302 is one of the lowest standards in the world, it still provides a minimum timeline for calculation of burn time. Polymerics and composites can burn slower but not faster than the minimum timeline of 102 mm per minute.

The latest form of the standard establishes some important classifications of the newer polymeric and nanocomposite plastics. The ability to identify these plastics when present in a burned vehicle is of paramount importance due to the fact that the newer plastics appear exactly the same as their earlier and much more flammable cousins. These classifications of the newer plastics are as follows.

> **does not ignite** (DNI). This material does not support the combustion during or following the 15-second ignition period and does not transmit a flame front across either surface to the first scribed line (fire snuffs out before 60 seconds).
> **self-extinguishing** (SE). This material ignites on either surface, but the flame extinguishes itself before reaching the first scribed line.

self-extinguishing/no burn rate (SE/NBR). This material stops burning before it has burned for 60 seconds from start of ignition, and has not burned more than 50.8 mm.[34]

The only significant difference to be noted in the testing method prescribed by J369 in comparison with the testing method prescribed by FMVSS 302 is that J369 requires that the testing fixture hold the sample material to be burned in a horizontal fashion whereas FMVSS 302 requires vertical testing. Other than that, the testing methodology is technically equivalent.

As a bit of standards reference trivia, SAE J369 is technically equivalent to ISO 3795. These standards are virtually verbatim to each other. The content of ISO 3795 will not be explored in this book.

The advent of automotive materials that will not ignite, will not support flame, and are self-extinguishing seems to fly in the face of the safety engineers at NHTSA. Some engineers might argue that the government moves a bit too slowly in reviewing FMVSS 302. Part of the reason is the cost of these newer materials. If FMVSS 302 were modified to be the technical equivalent of the applicable SAE J369 or other similar standards, then this would add significantly to the cost of an automobile as required by law.

The problem at this junction is for the engineer to be able to properly identify these newer composites. This is accomplished by a code which will be found cast into the plastic itself. This code is established in SAE J1344. It should be noted that the early and much more flammable plastics appear exactly the same to the naked eye as do the later (virtually) nonflammable polymerics.

2.4 Society of Automotive Engineers Standard J1344

The Society of Automotive Engineers has always moved to study safety issues in the ground transportation industry. Any SAE standard which begins with the letter "J" is designated as a ground transportation standard.

SAE Standard J1344 was first issued in October 1980. Primarily, this standard was issued for three purposes: First, the standardizing identification of plastic parts in response to ISO 14004. The era of recycling was sweeping across Europe and many other nations. There arose a need to create a system whereby the old scrapped-out automobiles could be stripped of their recyclable materials and the materials could be sorted into piles of matching plastics.

Second, the standard identification codes for plastic was in response to the need to standardize proper identification of all the types of plastic materials used in automobiles. Also, the identification codes allow an engineer to determine the flammability characteristics.

Third, the coding system allows repair professionals to determine if the part with which they are working can be repaired and repainted.

Section 4.1.7 establishes the accepted coding indicator when used with the materials tables contained in the standard.

Some examples of these are as follows:

>PP<	polypropylene
>PA66<	polyamide 66
>ABS + PC<	acrylonitrile/butadiene/styrene + polycarbonate blend[34]

If the investigating engineer removes a section of interior plastic on any given modern vehicle, there should be something similar contained in header marks "> <" or merely letters representing the blend cast into the mold without the header marks. It should be noted that the earlier version of SAE J1344 as issued in 1980 enclosed the code letters in a square box.

Thus, if the manufacturer follows the recommended practice in SAE J1344 the type of polymeric composite can be identified. From this the burn resistance of the material can be deduced.

2.5 International Standards Organization Number 14004

ISO 14004 was first passed in September 1996. Essentially, this standard was the first complete outline for a manufacturer to create and maintain a recycling system. This standard had several goals to managing and minimizing environmental impact in the manufacture and disposal of automobiles.

The main societal force behind ISO 14004 was from Europe. One by one, the individual nations were enacting laws which held the manufacturer responsible for the disposal of their automobiles. Rapidly, the country where the vehicle was made was becoming the country where the vehicle had to be disposed. It is obviously cost prohibitive to tow all junked automobiles back to the country that they were manufactured in. Hence, guidelines for recycling were needed.

ISO 14004 also addresses the disposal of hazardous materials. It establishes an identification system for such materials, embodies life cycle thinking in engineering departments, prevents pollution, reduces waste in the consumption of resources, and creates feasible disposal methods. For example, some trunk lamp assemblies utilize a mercury switch, or certain materials may contain lead in their makeup. With virtually universal material codes, the proper identification and handling protocols can be established for disposal.[21]

In the analysis of fire behavior in automobiles, ISO 14004 is merely another tool to assist in the proper identification of materials. As noted above, once the materials which comprise the burned vehicle are identified, then any conversion factors can be noted and BTU load calculations can be made.

2.6 International Standards Organization Number 1043-1

The scope of this standard is to establish and expand the SAE J1344 standard. ISO 1043-1 was first issued in May 1987 and reissued in December 2001. This standard provides abbreviated terms for the basic polymers and their special characteristics used in plastics, symbols for components of these terms, and symbols for special characteristics of plastics. It expands the equivalent SAE standard by including the newer polymeric and nanocomposites in the symbol system. The identification system is identical to the SAE J1344. This standard merely expands the number of materials included in the abbreviation codes. In the analysis of fire behavior this standard is included because it will contain some codes which are not contained in SAE J1344.[21]

2.7 International Standards Organization Number 1043-2

This standard is the second of four standards in the ISO 1043 series. The ISO 1043-2 standard was passed in May 2000. This standard provides uniform symbols for terms referring to fillers and reinforcing materials found in automotive plastics. It includes only those symbols that have come into established use. The main aim is both to prevent the occurrence of more than one symbol for a given filler or reinforcing material and to prevent a given symbol being interpreted in more than one way. As with the other standards, this utilizes the same format as set forth in SAE J1344. This standard merely addresses the fillers and reinforcement materials used.

The reason that this standard is important is that some fillers, when added to a given plastic, will render that plastic less flammable. However, the fillers and reinforcement materials covered in this standard are not classified as flame retardant. The truly flame retardant materials classifications are contained in ISO 1043-4.[21]

If the investigating engineer is analyzing the BTU potential of a given plastic, he or she will need to know if that plastic is more difficult to ignite, whether or not the filler will retard the transfer temperature characteristics of the material, and the correct identification of what the material is comprised from. If he or she has only SAE J1344 symbols and abbreviations to work from, then the code on the piece being examined may not appear on the SAE list. Hence, this will confound proper identification and may lead to improper analysis.

2.8 International Standards Organization Number 1043-4

This standard regards fillers used as fire retardants. It was issued in May 2000. This standard furthers the codes and abbreviations used on newer polymerics and nanocomposites. The coding indicator of header markings "> <" is the same as the SAE J1344. The biggest difference is how the flame retardant materials are coded into the plastic casting. Some examples are as follows.

> **Example 1.** For a polypropylene containing 30 percent by mass of mineral power, use >PP-MD30<.
>
> **Example 2.** For a polyamide 66 containing a mixture of 15 percent by mass of mineral powder and 25 percent by mass of glass fiber, use >PA66-(GF25+MD15)< or >PA66-(GF+MD)40<.
>
> **Example 3.** For a polyamide 66 containing a mixture of 15 percent by mass of mineral powder and 25 percent by mass of glass fiber and, additionally, red phosphorous 52 as a flame retardant, use >PA66(GF25+MD15)FR(52)< or >PA66-(GF+MD)40FR(52)<.[21]

The newer polymerics and nanocomposites have a percentage of their molecular makeup from nonflammable material such as glass beads, talcum and many others. The nonflammable materials are actually embedded into the plastic such that their appearance is exactly as the older plastics with the higher volatile organic compounds content. This subject will be covered in more detail later.

2.9 International Standards Organization Number 1629

This standard establishes the nomenclature, symbols, and abbreviations for rubber and lattices found in automotive rubber products as well as other nonautomotive plastics. This standard was first issued in November 1995. The ISO 1629 standard establishes classification for different types of rubbers. These groupings are as follows:

> **M.** Rubbers having a saturated carbon chain of the polymethylene type.
> **N.** Rubbers having carbon and nitrogen in the polymer chain.
> **O.** Rubbers having carbon and oxygen in the polymer chain.
> **Q.** Rubbers having silicon and oxygen in the polymer chain.
> **R.** Rubbers having an unsaturated carbon chain (i.e., natural rubber and synthetic rubbers derived at least partly from conjugated dienes).
> **T.** Rubbers having carbon, oxygen, and sulfur in the polymer chain.
> **U.** Rubbers having carbon, oxygen, and nitrogen in the polymer chain.
> **Z.** Rubbers having phosphorus and nitrogen in the polymer chain.[21]

The reason for proper identification of the rubber products present in the automobile being analyzed is that the flammability characteristics vary drastically among some of the classifications.

For example, if pyrolyzed carbon is on the underside of a wooden bed plank for a truck which has suffered a fire, then it can be deduced that the daily coating of carbon black and polybutadiene from worn tire dust (coats all roads) contributed to the rapid spread of the flames. If compared with the rubber makeup of an air conditioning hose there is a drastically different flammability factor. The investigating engineer will need to understand the differing properties of rubber flammability to arrive at a correct diagnosis confidently.

2.10 International Standards Organization Number 11469

This standard is the technical equivalent of SAE J1344. However, as noted above, the International Standards Organization has a history of more prompt review of the accuracy and keeping abreast of new industry developments. Hence, their standards should always be included in any research on automotive materials.

This standard was first issued in March 1993. The second edition was reissued in May 2000. It includes additional generic identification and marking requirements for plasticizers and flame retardants. The standard also expanded the marking methodology from cast only to melt imprinting and indelible marking. Another change in this standard is that it established a method for marking products with two or more components which are difficult to separate.

Example. A product made of three components, the visible one being a thin coating of polyvinyl chloride over a polyurethane containing an insert of acrylonitrile-butadiene-styrene which is the major component by mass, is marked >PVC,PUR,ABS<.

A code found on a piece of plastic may be contained in one standard but overlooked in another. Prudent research protocols require the proper identification of the polymeric in question.

2.11 *Deutsch Institut für Normung* Number 260

The *Deutsch Institut für Normung* (DIN) is the German equivalent of the Society of Engineers. The only difference is that their standards apply to vehicles of European origin. Germany has been the traditional leader in the recycling of scrap materials. The focus of DIN/VDA Standard Number 260 is the technical equivalent of SAE J1344.[10]

As noted above, if the automobile fire investigation turns up a piece of polymeric plastic on a vehicle that cannot be identified using the codes contained in the other related standards, the material code may apply only to European vehicles and might be found in this standard.

2.12 American Society of Testing and Materials Standard 1600

The American Society of Testing and Materials (ASTM) Standard 1600 is another technical equivalent of SAE J1344. This standard was issued in February 2000. The previous edition of the standard was issued in 1998.

This standard differs from SAE J1344 and SAE J369 in that the list of flame retardant compounds and additive polymerics are classified by a numeric system. This numeric system is contained in Section 7.1.1.1 of ASTM Standard 1600.

Table 2.1 contains the numeric codes used in the plastic industry for non-flammable materials bonded to other polymerics. This code differs in that it is a numeric code not an letter code.

2.13 International Standards Institute Standards Numbers 472 and 1087

The ISO numbers 472 and 1087 are germane to this research in that these documents establish agreed-on definitions for the worldwide plastics industry. These two standards were first issued in 1990 and reissued in November 1999. Both standards are published in English and French to reduce the confusion encountered when terms are translated into different languages.

2.14 Conclusion

In analyzing the vehicle fire, the first step the investigating engineer should take is an appraisal of the types of polymeric composite plastics available for consumption at the core of the fire. If the entire vehicle has been consumed, this may require procuring a similar make and model for disassembly and parts identification. The question to be answered at this junction is whether the fire was consistent with the ability of the on-board plastics to transfer heat and flaming combustion.

As previously discussed, the different varieties of plastics may look and feel quite similar. The investigating engineer must be able to properly identify the consumed plastic or rubber component and be able to determine that type of material's propensity for sustaining a flame front. A solid understanding of the applicable codes and standards for that product allows the analysis to be made with confidence. If the investigation has uncovered a piece of material which contains a code which is not contained in one standard, then all of the standards must be searched until the material is identified.

FMVSS 302 code only applies to any plastic, composite, or polymeric that is within 13 mm (about 0.5 inch) of the passenger compartment air space. By placing a cover shield over the lower portion of the steering column and across the lower portion of the dashboard, most modern vehicles have now separated the "air space" of the passenger compartment from the internal components of the dashboard. These cover shields allow the manufacturer to use a more flammable type of plastic to construct the dash components. One point to note here is that the plastic cowlings that surround steering column ignition switches are often constructed from flame retardant polymerics, while the dash shield next to it will not be. This is because of the potential of fire from the ignition switch area. Some manufacturers construct the ignition switch body from porcelain to reduce fire hazard. The greatest concentration of components capable of being the cause of fire in the passenger compartment are located inside the dashboard.

A second area of analysis of FMVSS 302 that should be considered by the investigating engineer is that this standard does not apply to any of the plastics located in the engine compartment or trunk. If the manufacturer chooses to construct the vehicle from less-flammable materials, then that is an allowable practice, not a required one. As a general rule, the more flammable plastics are found on entry-level vehicles for any given manufacturer. This is because these plastics are more cost-effective from which to produce parts. The less-flammable polymeric composite and nanocomposite cousins are equipped on the higher-trim and luxury levels of automobiles.

FMVSS 302 should be considered the bare minimum standard by which any automobile can be sold in the U.S. market. The investigating engineer can deduce the approximate level of destruction of the existing types of composites by analyzing the fire department report. The time from reporting to final extinguishment will be contained therein. Automobile fires generate tremendous amounts of acrid smoke and, generally, attract attention quickly. In most urban areas, fire department response time is approximately 10–15 minutes from any given location in that city.[13]

Table 2.1
ASTM D 1600, Section 7.0: Code Numbers for
Identifying Flame Retardant Compounds

7.1.   The code numbers are grouped according to the chemical
          composition of the flame retardant.

7.1.1.1. Halogenated Compounds: In compounds containing both
          aliphatic/alicyclic and aromatic groups, the group containing
          the halogen determines the code to be used.

Code   Compound
10   aliphatic/alicyclic chlorinated compounds
11   aliphatic/alicyclic chlorinated compounds with antimony
          compounds
12   aromatic chlorinated compounds
13   aromatic chlorinated compounds in combination with
          antimony compounds
14   aliphatic/alicyclic brominated compounds
15   aliphatic/alicyclic brominated compounds with antimony
          compounds
16   aromatic brominated compounds (excluding brominated
          diphenylether and biphenyls)
17   aromatic brominated compounds in combination with
          antimony compounds
18   polybrominated diphenylether

19   polybrominated diphenylether in combination with antimony
          compounds
20   polybrominated biphenyls
21   polybrominated biphenyls in combination with antimony
          compounds
22–24   not allocated
25   aliphatic fluorinated compounds
26–29   not allocated

7.2.   Nitrogen Compounds
30   nitrogen compounds (including but not limited to melamine,
          melamine cyanurate, urea
30–39   not allocated

Table 2.1 (continued)

7.3.   Organic Phosphorous Compounds
40   halogen free organic phosphorous compounds
41   chlorinated organic phosphorus compounds
42   brominated organic phosphorous compounds
43–49   not allocated

7.4.   Inorganic Phosphorous Compounds
50   ammonium orthophosphates
51   ammonium polyphosphates
52   red phosphorous
53–59   not allocated

7.5.   Metallic Oxides, Hydroxides, and Salts
60   aluminum hydroxide
61   magnesium hydroxide
62   antimony (III)-oxide
63   alkali antimonite
64   magnesium/calcium carbonatehydrate
65–69   not allocated

7.6.   Boron and Zinc Compounds
70   inorganic boron compounds (excluding zinc borate)
71   organic boron compounds
72   zinc borate

73   inorganic zinc compounds (excluding zinc borate)
74   not allocated

7.7.   Silica Compounds
75   inorganic silica compounds
76   organic silica compounds
77–79   not allocated

7.8.   Miscellaneous Compounds
80   graphite
81–89   not allocated
90–99   not allocated

Source: ASTM Technical Standard D-1600, 2000[1]

Chapter 3

Automotive Fire Mechanisms

   B. Low burn patterns
   C. Melted pools of glass
   D. Extreme consumption of polymerics
   E. Fire burning under engine or floor pan
   F. Fire in different compartments
   G. Destruction of steering column
   H. Destruction of large aluminum castings
3.11 Alternative Technology
   A. Bi-fuel vehicle
   B. Flex-fuel vehicle
   C. Compressed Natural Gas
   D. Liquid Natural Gas
   E. Gas-electric hybrid vehicles
   F. Fuel cell vehicles
   G. Lithium-ion batteries
        1. Failure modes
   H. Supplemental restraint systems and Event Data Recorders
   I. Golf cart fires

3.1 Fire Behavior Basics

Fire is similar to something that is alive. All types of fire will extinguish if deprived of either oxygen, fuel, or sufficient space in which the flame structure can form. Fire will tend to display a certain propensity of behavior in similar given situations. However, automobiles will add many more mechanisms for fire initiation and propagation than structure fires. The behavior of automotive fire is distinctly different from structure fire behavior.

The first law of thermodynamics is that heat will flow from an exothermic environment into an endothermic environment. The area of greater heat will always spread into or onto the area of lesser heat provided there are no impediments to the normal propagation of the heat.

Early automobiles were constructed of some very combustible materials. Solid materials such as wood, polyvinyl chloride tops and seat covers, cotton pad and batting, mohair, household velour upholstery fabrics, along with organic and inorganic compounds were found on automobiles from inception through 1970. If the car caught fire, the chances for a large and flaming total loss were excellent. As previously discussed, the materials and plastics from which an automobile is constructed became steadily less combustible as the years passed.

The most common areas for an automobile to start a fire are from the engine compartment or from under the dashboard. Underhood fires are more likely to start out as a larger order fire than dashboard fires due to the presence of flammable or combustible liquids. If one or more of the flammable liquids ignites, then an area of positive pressure will be created in the engine compartment. Depending on the amount and type of flammable liquid burning, a positive pressure of +3 to +4 psia, where atmosphere = 1, will be created (measurements taken by this author, 2002). PSIA stands for "pounds per square inch of the area (or atmosphere)." If the Earth's atmospheric pressure at sea level is considered to equal one, then the high release rate of the burning flammable liquids creates a ball of heated air (heat plume) which has higher air pressure than the non-heated air. This positive pressure will tend to push the flames outward and possibly downward. Understanding this concept allows the investigating engineer to distinguish why a burn pattern was directed to a low point on the vehicle when fire naturally burns upward.

Most automobiles are designed with compartments. The engine is a sealed compartment separate from the passenger compartment. The trunk is a sealed compartment separate from both the engine and passenger compartments. The investigating engineer will need to understand how the compartments are sealed off from each other to answer the question of how the propagation of the flame front occurred. Explanation of the air entrainment through a vehicle fire will differ from a structure due to configuration of the compartments.

The next area of basic fire behavior to be examined is the burn temperature and the burn pattern. The questions to be answered here are what part of the vehicle did the fire originate in, how hot did it get, and how did it spread. Fire must demonstrate a path. It cannot simply jump gaps or display unusual attributes unless forced to by outside influences such as cargo or an accelerant.

For example, many late model Ford pickup trucks have the entire A/C evaporator, heater core, and blower motor all located inside the passenger compartment. Except for the small holes where the A/C tubing and the heater core tubing penetrate the firewall, the steering column, and the union plugs for the wiring, the engine compartment is virtually a solid steel wall. If the investigating engineer sees a burn pattern inside the passenger cabin area when the fire initiated underhood, then he or she must find an answer as to how and why the fire penetrated the firewall.

If the investigating engineer encounters a situation where the fire behavior has not followed explainable patterns, then that investigation must be approached with the possibility of incendiary fire causation in mind. A proper conclusion of incendiary fire should only be reached after eliminating all other possibilities.

3.2 Exhaust System Fires

The exhaust system on automobile and trucks is the hottest structure anywhere on the vehicle. This obviously has the greatest potential for causing a fire should some unwanted combustible material or flammable liquid come in contact with a hot exhaust.

The temperature of the exhaust manifold will vary with the design of the automobile. Most engines do not create enough heat at the exhaust manifold or other components of the exhaust immediately after start-up to cause any kind of fire regardless of what flammable liquid the surface is exposed to. However, some of the later systems such as the Bosch Motronic® system will use a unique adaptive strategy for the engine warm-up cycle. This type of system will create the heat necessary for auto ignition of any flammable liquid shortly after start-up. These systems will move the timing to the fully retarded position and raise the idle during the warm-up cycle. The purpose of this is to shorten the catalytic converter light-off time by forcing the engine to create extremely hot exhaust gasses when the engine is cold.[4]

If the case at hand involves a fire which started immediately after cold start-up, then this must be explained. Given an ambient air temperature of 70°F most engines require an operating time of 10–20 minutes before auto ignition capability is reached. For example, a hypothetical late model Mercedes Benz is capable of generating sufficient heat in the exhaust system within 30 seconds of start-up to cause a burst power steering to auto ignite whereas a similar model Chevrolet will not. This is due to the adaptive strategy of the Bosch Motronic® system. As of the date of this study, GM does not use the cold start/full retard adaptive strategy on any of its models. Many models after 2002 have adapted this start-up strategy. The investigating engineer should always check the correct workshop manual for the configured adaptations of the system.

Starting with the combustion chamber inside the engine, the average operating temperature after the engine is warm is approximately 2,000–2,300°F. If combustion chamber temperatures exceed 2,300–2,500°F then the engine will begin forming nitrogen oxide gasses (NOx).[35]

The OBD I and II engine computers can potentially yield usable information on engine overheat conditions provided that the communication system is intact enough to retrieve any operating fault codes. All vehicles built for sale in the U.S. market after 1991 are Onboard Diagnostics I (OBD I) compliant. Vehicles built after 1996 are OBD II compliant. The OBD I and OBD II programs are specified in the SAE Standards J1969 and J1972, respectively. [34]

The engine data stream and fault codes for OBD II vehicles are all identical regardless of manufacturer. This information is retrieved using a tool known as a "scanner." If the vehicle is an OBD I, the connector is unique to each manufacturer. The scanner tool kit contains all the necessary adaptors and software to interrogate the system. If the vehicle is an OBD II vehicle, the Assembly Line Data Link (ALDL) connector is identical in all vehicles. The OBD II connector is a 16-pin D-style connector which must be located within 18 inches of the vehicle centerline and is accessible to a crouching technician with no tools.

For example, if the scanner tool reveals that there were multiple misfires and an overheat code stored, it can be interpreted that the engine was having operational problems which may have contributed to the part failure that caused the fire. Misfiring in the engine typically causes the catalytic converter to overheat. Over the years, this author has observed catalytic converters and exhaust systems glowing red-hot on malfunctioning vehicles. An occasional catalytic converter with a melted core has also been observed. See Figure 3.1 for a melted catalytic converter.

The engine management system is designed to detect the production of NOx or excessive hydrocarbons and adjust the engine's operating parameters to reduce tailpipe emissions. The engine management system will always attempt to adjust the combustion mixture to a 14.7:1 ratio. This is the optimal fuel-to-air mixture which will promote the lowest emission levels of hydrocarbons (HC), carbon monoxide (CO) and oxides of nitrogen (NOx). The ratio of 14.7:1 is known as the "stochiometric ratio." See section 3.2.D.1, *Gasoline*, below for a more detailed discussion on engine management systems.

As the exhaust gasses leave the cylinder head into the exhaust manifold some of the hot gas energy will be used to heat the manifold itself while the remainder of the gasses will proceed down the exhaust pipe.

The surface temperature of the exhaust manifold will vary according to the thickness of the manifold, the ambient air temperature, and valve overlap fac-

Figure 3.1 *Melted catalytic converter*

tors inherent in engine design. As noted above, heat will always move from the exothermic environment to the endothermic environment. The extremely hot exhaust gasses will heat the manifold which in turn gives off heat to the ambient air. The average operating temperature of the surface of an exhaust manifold is approximately 500–1,000°F when the ambient air is approximately 75°F. On malfunctioning engines, exhaust manifold temperature can reach as high as 1,600°F. The transfer temperature of the exhaust system will drop as the heated exhaust air travels down the exhaust pipe.

The ambient air temperature inside the engine compartment as measured at center of the underside of the hood will vary from ambient outside air temperature before start-up to a high of 300°F+. The closer to the surface of the exhaust manifold the air temperature is measured, the higher the ambient air readings will be.

It should be noted that cast iron and stainless steel exhaust manifolds will begin to glow red-hot starting at around 1,200°F. Melting point for most iron and steel is approximately 2,000–2,800°F. The melting point of steel varies dramatically with the presence of carbon, nickel, and chromium. Any steel with an alloy of a minimum of 11.5 percent chromium is considered a stainless steel.[6] A simple test for the presence of stainless steel exhaust components is to use a magnet. Lower grades of stainless steel will display limited magnetic properties. Higher grades of stainless steel are nonmagnetic.

The next part of a modern exhaust system is the catalytic converter. The normal internal operating temperature of a catalyst is around 1,200–1,400°F. Most designs of this device incorporate a long honeycomb made of porcelain with an outer skin made of stainless steel. The porcelain core is coated with platinum, palladium, and rhodium. A modern catalytic converter is known as a three-way catalyst. The catalyst bed is sometimes referred to as a "monolith."

Functioning normally, the outer skin temperature of a catalytic converter on a modern vehicle will run around 500–800°F given that the catalytic converter is located no more than 4–5 feet from the exhaust manifold. Sometimes the catalytic converter is mounted directly to the exhaust manifold. In this configuration, the skin temperature will be the same as the exhaust manifold.

Many catalytic converter systems incorporate an extra tube which injects fresh air taken from the air cleaner area into the exhaust stream just before the catalytic converter. This system will promote cleaner burning inside the catalyst core. The effect on operating temperature of the catalyst is minimal.

There are two main reasons that the catalyst outer skin temperature can vary so drastically during normal operation: first, engine running condition will dramatically affect catalytic converter performance; second, partial catalyst failure can be caused by clogging. As a catalytic converter gets older some of the hon-

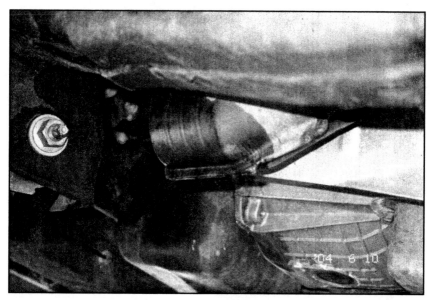

Figure 3.2

Figure 3.3

eycomb passages will coat over or plug altogether with exhaust carbon rendering part of the catalyst bed ineffective. If the engine is running rough with several cylinders running too rich or not firing, this will cause the unburned hydrocarbons to enter the catalytic converter. The extra rich fuel mixture will cause the catalytic converter to overheat. A rough-running motor can cause the catalytic converter skin temperature to rise as high as 1,600°F. At this temperature, the catalytic converter is glowing bright red-hot.

Figure 3.2 depicts an exhaust fire. In this case the power steering fluid ruptured over the hot exhaust and catalytic converter. There is an oil residue visible on the surface of the catalytic converter.

Some signs of an overheated catalytic converter would be scorched floor insulation padding, melted or scorched elastomeric floor coatings, and burned or discolored paint inside the cabin area directly above the catalytic heater. Another sign of an overheated catalytic converter is if the core has melted. Removal of the catalytic converter is required to view the melted core. A melted core inside the catalytic converter indicates that exhaust gas temperatures were in excess of 3,000°F in the operating timeframe before the loss.

This type of evidence can be misinterpreted. It is possible that the engine being examined had operational problems whereby the catalytic converter core had partly melted several months or even years prior to the fire occurrence. The engine was repaired and the failed catalytic converter had not been spotted as a problem as it was still allowing air to pass through. Thus, the evidence looks like the engine was currently overheating but in reality it was not.

There are two other locations on the engine where the extreme exhaust temperatures can be encountered. The first is known as the "exhaust crossover." The second is an "exhaust gas recirculation" (EGR) valve.

The exhaust crossover is a passage generally found on V-style carbureted engines. Essentially it is a separate tunnel which runs from the center of each head through the intake manifold. It expands in size directly under the carburetor mounting area. The purpose of the exhaust crossover is to preheat the air-fuel mixture as it enters the intake runners. The exhaust crossover does not mix with the air-fuel mixture. The system causes a separate chamber to heat up which in turn heats the air-fuel mixture as it flows over the intake manifold runners. Many times this exhaust crossover will plug up and no longer be effective. This may have an effect on catalytic converter skin temperature due to increased HC production.

The EGR valve is a device typically bolted to the intake manifold. However, it can be mounted elsewhere on the engine. All designs of this device have one passage which leads from the exhaust up to a valve. The second passage leads to the intake manifold. The valve is either vacuum activated or actuated via electric solenoid. When the engine management system opens the valve, this allows a small amount of the exhaust gas back into the intake air-fuel mixture. This reduces combustion chamber temperatures by introducing an inert gas into the air-fuel mixture. The surface temperature of the valve is the same as the exhaust manifold although it may not be located anywhere near the exhaust manifold.

The investigating engineer should remove the intake manifold and the EGR valve when the suspected point of origin is the top of the engine to determine if the subject vehicle is functioning within specifications. If gasoline were to leak out of the carburetor onto the hot surface of the exhaust crossover, then a fire could occur much more readily than an intake manifold system which does not incorporate one or has a plugged exhaust crossover.

Similarly, if the EGR valve is not functioning correctly this can result in higher operating temperatures inside the combustion chamber, an engine "knock" or pre-detonation, or poor idle. Any of these conditions can cause a catalytic converter to overheat.

Caution should always be observed so that the true primary failed part is discovered. The primary failed part is not always the part that caused the fire to break out.

The next device in the exhaust system is the muffler. Some vehicles will also use a device closer to the end of the tailpipe called a resonator. A resonator looks much like a smaller version of the muffler. The muffler is a canister with a series of baffles surrounded by fiberglass insulation. The pipe connecting the catalytic converter and down to the muffler will measure approximately 400–500°F. The skin of the muffler will measure approximately 250–350°F.

As the exhaust system pipe gets further away from the engine, it will naturally give up more of its heat to the ambient air. The very tip of the tailpipe on most vehicles will measure approximately 250–300°F with an ambient air temperature of 70°F (all exhaust temperature measurements taken by this author, various models, 2002).

Some types of exhaust contact fires are as follows.

A. Foreign objects on the exhaust

If a road hazard such as a plastic bag or some type of cloth should wrap itself around any part of the exhaust system, there is a good chance that this might cause a fire to erupt. It does not matter if the vehicle is driving at freeway speeds. Flames are capable of auto ignition and propagation at freeway speeds when natural fibers or common plastics reach temperatures of approximately 350–450°F. If sufficient heat is trapped between the contacting material and the hot exhaust surface, including the muffler, freeway speeds will not blow the flames out (white tee-shirt test conducted by this author, 1999).

B. Truck bed floorboard fires from the exhaust

There is another type of exhaust fire which is a bit more unusual: the truck bed floorboard fire. This type of fire only occurs to medium-size trucks and pickup trucks with wooden plank style bed floorboards. The hazard occurs when the exhaust pipe has been routed too closely to the wooden floorboards or the wooden insulator between the bed itself and the top of the frame rails. Industry standard for the minimum distance the exhaust pipe mounting must be from a frame or wooden floorboard is 4 inches.[22]

One rare condition which may be encountered is the exhaust pipe being mounted fairly close to but not touching a wooden floorboard. Over a period of time a process known as "pyrolysis" will occur. This process causes the carbon molecules in the wood to begin a distillation and drying process that results in a carbon surface which can auto ignite at a much lower temperature and sustain glowing combustion once started. The process is much like making charcoal briquettes out of partially burned wood.

The scientific theory of pyrophoric carbon is not currently a viable legal theory even though a great deal of anecdotal evidence exists to support the existence of this phenomenon. In a recent case, *Truck Insurance Exchange v. MagneTek, Inc.*, expert testimony on the subject of pyrophoric carbon did not pass muster under a *Daubert* analysis. This is discussed in greater detail in Chapter 5.

Once a wooden floorboard fire has been initiated, the spread will be enhanced by the presence of worn tire dust and, quite possibly, a collection of fibers from past cargo. The tire dust is present on all roads. The underside of a vehicle is constantly re-coated with oily road grime containing worn tire dust. Also, fibers from cargo accumulate around the cracks between the floorboards. The tire dust is comprised of minute particles of neoprene, carbon black, styrene, and polybutadiene.[38]

The investigating engineer may encounter what seems to be a rather large fire spread pattern underneath a truck floor. The spread pattern will normally appear inconsistent with surface communication. This type of pattern could be caused by the fire spreading across the buildup of worn tire dust, wood preservative, and fibers accumulated on the underside of the floorboards. The type of cargo the truck normally carries should be investigated to determine the type of fibers which may be involved.

For example, if the flat bed truck is used for hauling carpet there may very well be an abundance of flammable fibers which have accumulated from the carpet pieces and carpet padding typically hauled during normal operations.

One reason the exhaust systems vary on stake bed and bobtail trucks is because the vast majority of these trucks are sold as a cab and chassis from the truck manufacturer. The truck bed is provided by an "upfitter" company. The exhaust system may have been modified as part of the upfitted bed process. Possibly, the builder has erroneously routed the new exhaust pipe too close to the truck bed wooden planks.

C. Underhood fluids

The normal fluids found in an engine compartment are transmission fluid, power steering fluid, engine oil, brake fluid, coolant, and windshield wiper fluid. It should be noted that some brands of windshield wiper fluid are flammable due to the high concentrations of alcohol. All of these fluids are capable of starting a fire if a leak occurs during operation and the fluid comes in contact with the hot exhaust. Brake fluid is the most easily combustible fluid from auto ignition.

It should be noted that most vehicle manufacturers will commonly ship a new vehicle from the factory with the coolant-to-water ratio at approximately 45-49 percent coolant. At this concentration the coolant will not catch fire if a rupture in the cooling system occurs. If the consumer lives in snow country, the selling dealer will usually test the coolant for proper freezing protection during the pre-delivery inspection. Most of the time coolant leaks will not catch fire unless the dealer or the owner of the vehicle has topped up the system with pure coolant such that the mixture exceeds 60 percent coolant-to-water ratio.[23]

Depending on the type of leak, a ruptured flammable liquid line can emit conditions ranging from a fine mist to a stream. There is also the operating pressure of the individual systems to consider. The average operating pressures which can be encountered by different designs are as follows.

- power steering with rack and pinion   75–400 psi
- power steering with conventional steering gear   600–1,200 psi
- automatic transmissions   75–110 psi
- fuel pump for carburetors   3–7 psi
- fuel pump for fuel injection   30–120 psi
- engine oil pressure   15–75 psi
- cooling systems   12–17 psi
- hydraulic ride or active ride control systems   125–1,800 psi
- operating pressures of brake system non-ABS   0–1,800 psi
- operating pressure of ABS brake system   0–2,200 psi
- diesel fuel injection-inline or rotary pump   350–3,000 psi
- diesel fuel injection-common rail   15,000–30,000 psi*

*(3D generation systems)

Note: Almost all gas fuel injection systems built after 1991 (OBD I) will operate on pressures which range from 40–48 psi. However, some older systems

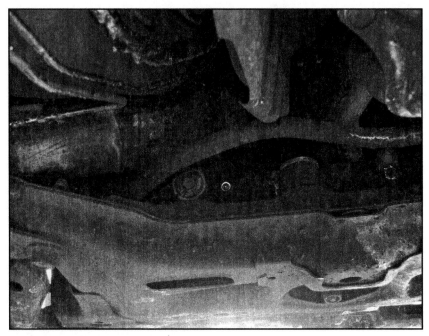

Figure 3.4 New style steering rack.

operated on higher pressures of up to 100 psi. For vehicles built after 1996 (OBD II), the pressure range of 30–48 psi became an industry standard.

As a footnote to power steering pumps, there is the advent of the power steering pump being mounted into the steering gear itself. The pump is powered by an electric motor. The pump and motor are encased in the same casing affixed to the steering gear. There may or may not be a power steering reservoir located above, depending on the manufacturer.

The design approach of using a self-contained electric power steering pump and steering gear allows the manufacturer to free up the horsepower drained from the engine by a fan belt driven pump. This approach also reduces the expense of power steering hoses, engine brackets to hold the power steering pump, and the warranty costs from hose failure. Also, eliminating a potential source of underhood operating mode fire from a power steering hose leak results in greater savings from fire claims. See Figure 3.4.

The investigating engineer should consult the OEM parts images of the system being inspected to determine if the electric power steering unit uses an external dipstick tube or fluid reservoir. Identification of one of the units is easily performed visually. The inquiry into the parts used in the system is performed to cover all bases and determine if any potential for fluid leaks exists.

An exhaust fire is usually the most damaging to the engine compartment. This is due to the fact that an exhaust fire usually involves a flammable or combustible liquid coming in contact with a hot exhaust. This will give the fire an immediate advantage as the BTU release from the flammable liquid will raise the temperature of surrounding composites and other flammable liquids to the levels necessary for combustion to begin.

If the level of destruction becomes too great, analysis for the primary failed part becomes difficult if not impossible. The best fires to analyze are the ones which have been extinguished quickly.

It should be noted that diesel fuel can auto ignite in a manner similar to gasoline. However, auto ignition conditions generally require a very hot exhaust component onto which a fairly small quantity of diesel fuel leaks. The chance for achieving auto ignition from a diesel leak is enhanced if the leak is in the form of an atomized spray. The chance of fire erupting on a diesel engine is considerably less than a comparable gasoline engine.

Modern diesel engines configured with a catalytic converter will engage a "re-gen" cycle. During this cycle raw diesel fuel is injected into the cylinders at bottom dead center. This will push raw hydrocarbons into the exhaust stream. The hydrocarbon molecules will attach to the soot and NOx particulate contaminants in the exhaust stream and will be consumed in the catalytic converter. One other issue with this type of configuration is the greater concentration of diesel fuel in the engine oil. The mix of diesel in the engine oil renders the oil more combustible.

Other approaches to control the NOx and soot from a diesel engine is the addition of uric acid. Vehicles configured with this system will typically have a second fill neck for the urea pellets located next to the diesel fuel tank filler neck. The driver will have to purchase a bottle of urea pellets from the local dealer and refill the urea pellet reservoir approximately every 7,500 miles or the engine will stop running until the reservoir is refilled.

Turbochargers are another source of auto ignition from a flammable liquid leak. All turbochargers are lubricated with engine oil in a full flow manner. Many units are also cooled with a circulating coolant from the radiator.

Many times the turbine fan blade shaft will snap in two or explode the turbo housing. The oil will immediately leak onto the hot exhaust chamber of the turbo and auto ignite. The result is that flaming oil will be spewed all over the engine and engine compartment due to the passing exhaust gas stream. This results in an accelerated fire spread rate through the engine compartment. Many times this type of turbocharger failure results in flaming oil exiting the turbocharger housing burning a round hole in the engine side of the radiator core while leaving the rest of the radiator relatively unscathed. When the turbocharger shaft explodes into pieces, the air-to-air charge condenser hose (large air inlet hose) is blown off. A column of oil and fire spews from the round opening of the turbocharger housing onto the engine side of the radiator. Thus, the round melt pattern is made in the radiator core directly in line with the turbocharger housing. Essentially, the failed turbocharger acts like a battlefield flame-thrower spewing flaming oil. The failed turbocharger will spew oil at engine oil pressure after turbo failure but before the engine stops running.

If a turbocharger failure is suspected, the pieces of the turbine shaft and turbo housing should survive any engine fire. The investigating engineer should look in the air intake and down the exhaust chamber or pipe for any remaining pieces of the turbines. This may require engine and exhaust system disassembly.

If a condition of built-up and coked oil deposits is discovered in the exhaust or intake chamber, then this is a sign that the turbocharger had oil leak problems in the timeframe prior to the catastrophic destruction. Normally, low engine power complaints will also be noted by the driver prior to turbocharger destruction.

There are two types of turbochargers: Fixed vane and variable vane. The fixed vane is self-explanatory. A variable vane design will commonly allow the exhaust vane to vary in pitch. This allows the engine management system to control the speed of the turbocharger so that intake manifold pressure efficiency is maximized. Some common control designs are pressure diaphragms, electric "stepper" motors, and engine oil servo-motors. The type of system employed in the vehicle being inspected and the position of the exhaust vanes should be recorded by the investigating engineer to assist in documenting exhaust temperature when overheat conditions are suspected.

If the vehicle being inspected was equipped with an exhaust pyrometer, the driver should be interviewed to determine if the driver was maintaining watch on the gauge. A pyrometer is generally not found on diesel cars, RV's, or light trucks. These are quite common on heavy truck diesel engines.

Diesel engines can overheat going up a long uphill grade with a heavy load on the vehicle. The exhaust manifold and pipes can get so hot that nearby combustible or flammable materials could potentially auto ignite. Many heavy truck exhaust manifolds are coated with a specialized coating or utilize a specialized alloy that reacts by changing its color when the normal operating temperature ranges are exceeded. The investigating engineer should check manufacturer engineering data for this possibility.

In conclusion, an exhaust fire will always be an operational mode failure or in a very short time period after engine shutdown. Tests have shown that the surface temperature of an exhaust manifold will actually increase immediately after engine shut down. This phenomenon is known as "heat soak."[35] However, within a matter of minutes after engine shut down, the exhaust system has cooled down below the threshold required for auto ignition.

If ignition has occurred shortly after start-up, then the workshop manual for that model automobile should be consulted to determine if that vehicle utilizes a quick warm-up routine in its adaptive strategy. Fire erupting just seconds after a cold engine starts is unusual. This type of operational mode failure can be considered suspicious. However, all possibilities must be explored before the investigating engineer makes any decisions that the fire might be incendiary.

D. On-board flammable and combustible liquids

The principle difference between a flammable and a combustible fluid is the flash point temperature for that fluid. For purposes of fire analysis both have much the same destructive capabilities as accelerants. The argument is a technical one as to the exact temperature required for auto ignition (i.e., since the operational mode failure is a chaotic event, simple analysis such as whether the leak was a drip or a spray cannot be resolved and, hence, are irrelevant when the fire evidence indicates that a fluid leak was the cause of the fire being investigated).

As mentioned earlier, there are several on-board flammable liquids on modern automobiles. Obviously, if any come in contact with a hot exhaust the potential for auto ignition is imminent. However, the question to separate at this junction is how much damage should the investigating engineer consider "normal" when the BTU potential for each given quantity and type of fluids is considered?

After the investigating engineer has determined the type of polymeric composites the vehicle being investigated is constructed from, he or she should have an approximate idea formed as to the type and level of destruction that the available BTU load is capable of producing.

The interpretation of fire debris evidence is a highly subjective practice. However, armed with accurate information and diagnosis techniques, the investigating engineer can establish the primary failed part with confidence.

For example, the average gallon of gasoline contains between 115,000 to 165,000 BTUs. Please note, if the BTU content is to be expressed in BTUs per pound then the gallon total is divided by six. On a modern automobile, the total BTU potential of all the available flammable and combustible liquids under the hood will not total anywhere near this figure. The average figure will calculate to somewhere between 20,000–30,000 BTUs. Additionally, as the fluid reservoirs are attacked some of the fluid burns while some drips down to the ground as a liquid. If the damage level is too extreme for the calculated BTU load of the available flammable liquids at the point of ignition, then this must be explained somehow or the investigation should begin focusing on incendiary factors.

1. Gasoline

Gasoline is a liquid with aromatic properties. The vapors from gasoline are highly flammable while liquid gasoline is not. When a pool of gasoline is burning, the liquid is forming a vapor level over the top of the pool. The vapors are being consumed by the flames not the liquid. Gasoline is formulated to contain hydrocarbons linked in hexagonal chains. This adds to the stability of the product. The two most common methods for measuring gasoline volatility are the Reid vapor pressure method and ASTM Method 86.30.

Early vehicles were equipped with a carburetor. Depending on design, there was approximately 1–1.5 cups of gasoline stored in the carburetor bowls. If the float valve became stuck on the carburetor, then flooding of gasoline would result. All carburetors are equipped with a tube extending from the bowl area to the airspace over the venturi opening. The purpose of this is to vent the carburetor fuel bowl and to allow any flooding gasoline to spill over into the engine.

Most carburetor systems will have a mechanical fuel pump which operates on an eccentric cam mounted on the engine. As noted above, these systems all operate on 3 to 7 psi. However, if any flooding and resultant fire occurred during operation, then the engine would keep running and spewing gasoline until the fire destroyed the engine's electrical system or the engine stopped running from too much raw fuel in the intake. The 1–1.5 cups or so of fuel would typically melt the carburetor casing and create a hot spot burn pattern on top of the engine. In this example, the center of the engine should show the greatest heat damage, a burn pattern of lesser damage radiating outward, and a single burn spot in the paint on top of the hood.

There is another potential addition of BTUs when a rupture occurs in the rubber fuel line that connects the fuel tank metal feed line to the engine mechanical fuel pump. Most models will exhibit a siphoning from the tank with a gravity feed pressure. A large pool of flaming gasoline will begin forming under the vehicle at the frame rail. If the steel fuel tank itself should begin to heat up from convective or radiant heat, the pressure inside the tank will increase from the expansion of the gasoline. This will in turn force more gasoline out of the leaking rubber fuel line at the engine. Almost all vehicle models will mount this mechanical fuel pump low on the engine. Should this situation occur, it generally produces a burn pattern on top and underneath the vehicle but not necessarily all the way back to the fuel tank.

The investigator should be familiar with spalling found in concrete. Spalling will occur if the vehicle with the leaking gasoline source is parked on a concrete slab. Spalling occurs when concrete is exposed to sudden high heat. A field of pock marks appears where chunks of concrete have blown away from the surface of the slab.

Spalling can also be found as an accidental course of business in welding and blacksmith shops, junkyards, muffler shops, and anywhere an oxy-acetylene torch is used to cut steel lying on concrete.

When the oxy-acetylene torch flame is turned toward the concrete slab, chunks of overheated concrete will begin popping out of the slab.

The investigator must correctly identify the source of any spalling that is present in the fire evidence.

It should be noted that there were some Japanese and European models in the late 1970s and early 1980s which used a carburetor and an electrical fuel pump. Those older models will have the electric fuel pump either in or near the fuel tank. Most fuel tanks of the era were constructed from steel. Only a few models were equipped with plastic fuel tanks.

By contrast, almost all OBD I and II vehicles will have an electric fuel pump inside the fuel tank. The pump is generally controlled by the engine fuel management computer.

There is a great deal of variance on the different fuel injection systems and pressures involved from the early systems to the modern vehicle. The first fuel injection system was a mechanical system manufactured by Rochester for GM in 1957. It had a very poor reception with consumers. Production ceased on the system after two years.

The first mass-produced fuel injection systems began appearing on the Volkswagen "pancake engine" products as early as 1965. This was the Bosch D-Jetronic system which was an option on the Squareback station wagon, Fastback coupe, and Notchback sedan models. This system was rather unsophisticated. The fuel pump continued to run until the key was turned off or power was interrupted. If a fuel line leaked and a fire erupted, the system would continue to spray gasoline all over the engine compartment until the fire destroyed the power. This might take as much as 3 to 5 minutes as the fuel pump was located in front just below the fuel tank.

By contrast, a modern OBD II compliant vehicle will cut the electricity to the electric fuel pump within 2 seconds after the engine stops rotating regardless of the position of the ignition key. When the computer loses the sensor input from the crankshaft position sensor because the crankshaft is no longer rotating, the system responds by turning off the fuel pump relay cutting the fuel flow. Thus, fuel leakage to feed a fire is minimal.

Modern vehicles will also have an *inertia sensor*. Inertia is the resistance to momentum. If the vehicle is impacted sufficiently or rolls over, then the inertia switch senses this and cuts power to the fuel pump automatically. This is a safety feature to reduce passenger injury from collision fire. Some high-line systems will also unlock all the doors, turn the interior lights on, and/or start the hazard lamps flashing when the inertia sensor trips and cuts power to the fuel pump after a rollover collision. Earlier vehicles are equipped with a manual-reset on the inertia switch. Some more modern models will reset the inertia switch electronically by cycling the key off, then back on for two key cycles.

FMVSS Number 301 deals with fuel system integrity in the post-crash situation. Essentially, the code stipulates that "fuel spillage shall not exceed 28 g from impact until motion of the vehicle has ceased, and shall not exceed a total of 142 g in the five minute period following cessation of motion. For the subsequent twenty-five minute period, fuel spillage during any one minute interval shall not exceed 28 g."[13] The NHTSA test speed for all collision testing under this code section is 35 mph.

There are two points for the investigating engineer to note. First, this code does not cover fuel leaks during normal operational mode. Second, after impact, the fuel tank is still allowed to leak. Given the highly flammable nature of gasoline vapors, if even a small quantity leaking at the tank were to catch fire, then complete tank emollition can be expected. When a collision is involved, it is not difficult to determine that the cause of the fire was a ruptured fuel tank. As noted above, the focus of this research is operational mode failure.

There are several physical properties of gasoline which the investigating engineer should be aware of. These are:

- One gallon of gasoline weighs an average of six pounds.
- One gallon of gasoline will produce thirty cubic feet of vapor at 70°F.
- One gallon of gasoline will raise 230 cubic feet of air to a lower flammability limit of 1.4 percent.
- One ounce of gasoline produces 0.234375 cubic feet of vapor.
- Gasoline vapor will not ordinarily rise to a greater height than three feet. It is heavier than air. The molecules of the hydrocarbon chains will tend to cling together in a low cloud when confined.
- The flash point of gasoline is –45°F.
- The ignition temperature of gasoline is approximately 500°F.
- The flammable limits of gasoline vapor in air (percent by volume) is an upper limit of 7.6 percent and a lower limit of 1.4 percent.
- The specific gravity of gasoline is 0.8 (SAE scale).
- The vapor density of gasoline where air = 1 is 3–4 psia.
- The boiling point of liquid gasoline is 100°F. Hard boiling point is achieved at approximately 400°F.
- The petroleum-producing companies in the U.S. market will change gasoline blends for winter and summer operation. This has a direct effect on vaporization rate.[7,32]

The first critical analysis path for the investigating engineer to determine is if the level of consumption is consistent with the amount of flammable liquids which have ruptured their systems and contributed BTUs to the fire. Not every flammable liquid will rupture with every engine fire. The investigating engineer should inventory the available fluids which have and have not contributed to the burn.

Second, the investigator must determine whether there was a pathway of fire communication across the engine compartment. This task is performed by taking inventory of the area of greatest destruction moving to the area of least construction. Gasoline and other flammable liquids will have tremendous potential for fire communication and spread.

The investigator's tip here is to be suspicious of total destruction beyond the ability of the available BTUs. Fire burn patterns are discussed in greater detail in Section 3.5.

2. Power steering fluid, transmission fluid, and hydraulic ride fluid

The next type of on-board combustible liquids are power steering fluid, transmission fluid, and hydraulic ride fluid. Unless the design specifies a synthetic or mineral based hydraulic oil, then Type A, Type F, Dexron®, Dexron/Mercon®, and full synthetic transmission fluids, are the most common fluids in commercial use. They will all have similar BTU characteristics. Hydraulic ride fluids will typically be mineral base with a BTU factor similar to that of transmission and conventional hydraulic fluids only with a similar auto ignition point. Full synthetic oils are not mineral based. However, they will auto ignite when exposed to temperatures greater than 800°F.

It should be noted that both power steering fluid and transmission fluid have the second greatest propensity for auto ignition of all underhood flammable liquids. In many vehicles, transmission fluid is used as power steering fluid. Gasoline will ignite more readily with a piloted ignition source than will transmission fluids. However, transmission fluids will auto ignite at a lower temperature than gasoline and will resist piloted ignition until flash point is reached.

Another area to consider is the nature of the suspected leak. Many times when a power steering, transmission, or hydraulic ride hose begins to leak, it will emit a mist or a small stream of fluid. This misting condition or tiny spray condition can be considerably more flammable if exposed to a hot exhaust than a large discharge. This is because the available form of the leaking fluid will reach its flash point much more readily than if the hose burst in two and a very large leak developed. By the time the fire is extinguished, this tiny leak will no longer be apparent or testable. Most of the time the rubber portion of the hose has been consumed or badly damaged.

The critical analysis path for the investigating engineer here is to have a basic understanding of the total BTU potential from different types of transmission and hydraulic fluids. When there is a suspected rupture during operational mode, spots of flashed off oil residue may be noticed on the suspected area of the exhaust where the fluid landed.

3. Brake fluid

The next underhood flammable liquid available for consumption is brake fluid. There are three types of brake fluid currently in automotive use. These are DOT type 3, DOT type 4, and DOT 5 synthetic. DOT 3 and DOT 4 brake fluids are amber in color. DOT 5 synthetic is purple. DOT 3 and 4 brake fluids will auto ignite more readily than other brake fluids. Also, most manufacturers will have a brake fluid reservoir that holds upwards of 1 quart of brake fluid. Once ignited, a flaming brake fluid reservoir will allow the underhood fire to become a "high order" fire rapidly.

DOT 3 and 4 brake fluids are mainly comprised of methol hydrate, glycerin, and a group of chemicals called "amines." Amines function to limit corrosion in the brake system. DOT 3 and 4 brake fluids are essentially an alcohol-based product. If laboratory analysis is performed, mineral oil contamination should not appear at any level.

The biggest difference between the two classifications is referred to as the "wet" and "dry" boiling points. The wet and dry boiling points of the brake fluids are as follows:

	Wet	Dry
DOT 3	284°F	401°F
DOT 4	311°F	446°F
Synthetic	333°F	513°F

DOT 5 synthetic does not contain alcohol elements. This fluid is a polymer chain with known compression, oxidation, and lubricant properties. One of the properties of all brake fluids is to absorb condensation from the system into suspension. The property to absorb moisture is called "hygroscopic." Hence, the reference to wet and dry boiling points.[34]

As noted above, brake fluid will auto ignite when it comes in contact with a hot exhaust. All brake fluids will resist piloted ignition unless brought to their flash points first.

It should be noted that the legal allowable composition of brake fluids for automotive applications is covered in FMVSS Number 116. The standard for brake hoses is covered in FMVSS Number 106.[13.]

4. Coolant

The next underhood flammable liquid is coolant. Coolant is sold in the U.S. market in several varieties: ethylene glycol, propylene glycol, OAT, and H-OAT.

Ethylene glycol is by far the most common coolant. It is most commonly dyed green. During normal use of the automobile, the coolant will lose some of the active ingredients to evaporation and conversion. As noted above, most automobile manufacturers will ship their vehicles with a coolant-to-water ratio of just under 50/50. This is done as a safety measure to lessen the potential for fire should a coolant hose leak or erupt. On most vehicles, the greatest quantity of low pressure rubber hoses are on the cooling system. Most of the hoses are located on or near the engine. This increases the chance for a leak to occur onto the exhaust. Hence, the precaution of manufacturers is to lessen the chance of fire from a coolant leak.[7]

Propylene glycol is not chemically from the same family as its cousin. However, it does have very similar properties of auto ignition when exposed to a hot exhaust. Propylene glycol is sold in many auto parts stores as an "environmentally friendly" alternative to ethylene glycol.

OAT and H-OAT coolant blends are found in modern vehicles. The acronym stands for "organic acid technology." H-OAT stands for "hybrid-organic acid technology." OAT coolants contain sebacate, 2-ethylhexanoic (2-EHA) acids, and other organic acids, but no silicates or phosphates like those commonly found in ethylene glycol blends. H-OAT will include a small amount of silicates or phosphates. The OAT and H-OAT coolant blends will commonly be dyed red, orange or pink.

The investigating engineer should be aware that some manufacturers will have specified proprietary coolant blends of OAT or H-OAT. There are also blends on the market that the coolant manufacturer claims are acceptable for use with any OAT or H-OAT coolant formula. Regardless, pure OAT and H-OAT coolant blends can auto ignite when exposed to temperatures of 300°–450°+F.[43] The percentage of water-to-coolant ratio and proprietary formulas will affect the ability to auto ignite.

Both ethylene glycol and propylene glycol will also auto ignite when exposed to a hot exhaust. However, the mixture needs to be nearly pure for auto ignition. If the water content in the coolant is over 30-40 percent then ignition is not likely. When coolant was purposely burned in testing, auto ignition was achieved at approximately 1,000°F. The flames produced were nearly colorless and of short duration (coolant auto ignition test performed by this author, 2000, various coolant brands). However, all coolant blends are not created equal. Pure propylene glycol and ethylene glycol coolant blends can potentially auto ignite at temperatures of 700°–800°F.

Again, the quantity of the leak is a factor. A small leak of fluid onto the exhaust can reach its flash point rapidly. A large leak onto the same exhaust component may well have the effect of cooling the exhaust component down because of the copious amount dumped onto the component.

The investigating engineer should take a sample of the remaining coolant for testing when a coolant leak is suspected of starting the fire. A simple tool for testing coolant-to-water ratio in the field is called a "refractometer."

A refractometer is a handheld optical device which utilizes a magnifying lens, a reflecting mirror, and a calibrated scale printed on a specially coated piece of glass. A drop of coolant is placed onto the mirror using an uncontaminated eye dropper or similar. The mirror is folded against the printed scale and then held up to a light source. The concentration of coolant will appear in the eyepiece as a separation of color on the printed scale. A refractometer is required to measure OAT and H-OAT coolant blends. Use of a specific gravity measuring tool will not work properly on the newer coolant blends. However, a specific gravity tool will work for older coolant blends.

One note of caution in using the coolant refractometer is to make sure that the test sample is from the coolant level of the engine. Many times the fire department will extinguish the fire using ordinary water. The coolant sample should be collected from the engine block drain or from an area inside the block where no water from the fire extinguishing could possibly have diluted the sample, or a false reading will result.

5. Engine oil

Engine oil is capable of starting a fire if exposed to a hot exhaust in sufficient quantity. Generally, engines do not leak sufficient quantities of oil to start a fire. If a mechanical breakdown occurs whereby an internal component of the engine is blown through the block, this may cause sufficient oil spray onto a hot exhaust to start ignition. The investigating engineer may find a quart of oil stashed in the corner of the engine compartment by the owner of the vehicle being inspected. This is usually a sign that the engine was leaking oil.

Most modern engines utilize a semi- or full synthetic oil. Semi-synthetic oils are a blend of mineral oil and synthetic oil. Full synthetic oils are not based from petroleum. Rather, the molecular chain is comprised from methane, polyalphaolefins, synthetic esthers, and other "gas-to-liquid" (GTL) proprietary formulas. The synthetic oils are grouped into differing categories depending on structure of the molecule.

Synthetic oils have advantages in cold-start lubrication, high thermal breakdown, and extended service life changes compared to mineral-based oils. Full synthetic oil formulas are capable of auto ignition. However, most formulas will only auto ignite at temperatures of greater than 800°F (auto ignition testing performed by this author, 2010). In lab testing of full-synthetic motor oil products, General Motors engineers achieved auto ignition as low as 625°F.[44]

The investigating engineer should inquire as to which type of oil the consumer was using in the engine or transmission prior to the fire when an engine oil leak is suspected as the source of the fire.

6. Fuel injection

There is a somewhat rare phenomenon which can occur to modern fuel injected automobiles which results in an explosion from inside the crankcase area. This scenario involves a malfunctioning fuel injector. Most fuel injection systems will hold pressure in the fuel rail when the engine is off. This will allow quick starts without having to wait for the fuel pump to bring the fuel rail up to operating pressure. If the system has a leaky injector, this allows the injector to bleed fuel into its cylinder. The raw fuel collects over a period of time in the engine oil by seeping past the engine rings on the affected cylinder. When the vapors reach a mixture anywhere near a stochiometric ratio, then the vapors will auto ignite from the heat on the backside of the pistons. This in turn causes a sudden rise in positive crankcase pressure. This will blow out oil fill caps, valve cover gaskets, and possibly the intake manifold end gaskets. In the process, oil is spewed out over the hot exhaust resulting in a fire.

If the investigating engineer encounters the unusual evidence described above, then a sample of oil should be taken and sent out for spectrochemical analysis. The presence of fuel concentrations of > 2 percent by volume is a solid indicator that the subject vehicle had a malfunctioning fuel injection system. Spectrochemical analysis will be discussed in greater detail in Section 5.4.

7. Air filters

Another type of somewhat rare fire occurs in the air filter housing. There are two mechanisms for this type of fire. First, engines have an operational mode phenomenon called "valve overlap." The only type of engine which does not display this phenomenon is a variable valve timing (VVT) engine.

Valve overlap occurs at the end of the exhaust stroke in four-stroke engines. Before the exhaust valve is fully closed, the adjoining intake valve begins to open. There is a point in the cycle where both valves are slightly off of their respective valve seats. This causes slight back pressure pulsations inside the intake manifold plenum which in turn causes the fuel and air to go back out the throttle body or carburetor momentarily. Further, the vacuum inside the intake manifold drops from a normal high of eighteen to twenty inches of vacuum (at sea level) to approximately two inches of vacuum when the accelerator pedal is depressed for full acceleration. This constant washing of air and fuel mixture leads to carbon buildup on the engine side of the throttle butterfly.

It is possible for a piece of this carbon accumulation to begin glowing combustion, break loose and land in the air filter element. This can result in a fire.

Another rare air filter fire is from the air filter sucking in a lit cigarette butt which has been carelessly discarded by another motorist. The lit cigarette butt lands on the paper element and starts a fire. Both of these air filter fires are rare fire types but they can and do happen.

8. Windshield washing fluid

Another type of on-board flammable liquid is non-freezing windshield washer fluid. The only type of windshield washing fluid which is flammable is one with a formula containing a high concentration of methyl alcohol. The most common types are fluids rated for -25°F and -50°F. The formulas which are based in ammonia and detergent mixed with water do not auto ignite. Alcohol content can be tested by using the specific gravity method, the metric alcohol content method, or the British "balling" scale. The only time windshield washing fluid is capable of starting a fire is when a quantity leaks onto a hot exhaust. However, auto ignition temperature is approximately 875°F.[45] None of the commercially available formulas will ignite from piloted ignition unless the flash point has been achieved. The flames will burn colorless to slightly orange. The duration factor is low.

9. PAG and refrigerant oils

Air conditioning systems all contain a lubricating oil. The older R-12 Freon systems would commonly utilize mineral-based oil. R-12 systems were phased out beginning in 1994. R-134a refrigerant systems replaced the older Freon systems. European vehicles are required to meet a more stringent standard with regard to ozone layer damage in the atmosphere. The new refrigerant being phased in is R-1234yf. As of the date of this edition, there are no requirements to use the R-1234yf refrigerant in vehicles sold for the U.S. market.

The R-1234yf refrigerant is mildly flammable. Because of this flammability propensity, a more robust evaporator design is required to ensure passenger safety in the event of a collision. The SAE has passed standard J-2842 for evaporator units that meet the new approved robust designs adopted by the SAE. Only evaporator units certified to meet the J-2842 requirements may be labeled with this designation.

One issue of safety regards counterfeit refrigerants. Refrigerants are expensive. The new R-1234yf refrigerant is slated to sell for upwards of $100 per pound retail. Currently, R-134 sells for $30–$50 per pound retail. Consequently, there is strong motivation to counterfeit both R-134 and R-1234yf.

The biggest safety issue for the investigator would be if he or she were to inspect a vehicle that had counterfeit refrigerant where the system did not rupture in the fire. A common counterfeit refrigerant is R-40 (methyl chloride). This refrigerant will react when exposed to aluminum. The system could potentially rupture, exposing the investigator to a gas that could burn the lungs, eyes, and skin.

One of the issues is that the R-134a and R-1234yf molecule would not attach to the mineral-based oils to circulate the oil through the system. The first lubricant of choice by automobile manufacturers was Polyalkalyene Glycol (PAG) oil. Low cost was the driving factor. Polyol Ester (POE) oil was a later development. Both are in use by automobile and equipment manufacturers.

Belt-driven AC compressors in R-134 systems will commonly be equipped with PAG oil because it is the cheapest to manufacture. Hybrid air conditioning systems where the compressor is powered by an electric motor mounted to the compressor must be equipped with POE oils. POE oils will also work in R-134 systems. However, POE oils are more expensive.

When inspecting a R-1234yf system, the investigator will see a configuration of hoses that is different than both R-12 and R-134 systems. The R-1234yf system will be equipped with an Internal Heat Exchanger (IHX). The IHX is located between the liquid and low-pressure sides of the AC system. The purpose of the IHX is to transfer heat from the liquid line to the low-side line that routes to the compressor inlet. This ensures a full column of cooler liquid refrigerant to the expansion valve.

Another feature of R-1234yf AC systems is that they are not as efficient as R-134 systems. It is possible to retrofit R-134 into a R-1234yf system but that will not make it any more efficient. The R-1234yf system is simply a less efficient design. The sole advantage of these systems is less damage to the ozone layer should any refrigerant escape.

Final decision regarding the refrigerant issue is pending. However, the phase-in of the R-1234yf will likely be inevitable. The investigating engineer should inquire as to which type of refrigerant and oil is equipped in the air conditioning system on the vehicle being tested.

Refrigerant oils will attach to the refrigerant molecule and circulate throughout the air conditioning system. There will also be an accumulation of refrigerant oil at the compressor. One service issue on older vehicles or vehicles that have had the air conditioning serviced or recharged several times is the propensity for the technician to add a little oil when the system is recharged. If too much oil is present inside the system, then the excess will tend to collect in the lowest part of the system. Generally, this is the condenser.

Air conditioning systems will always have some pressure in the system regardless if the compressor is on or not. The refrigerant tends to be approximately equal in pressure as the outside ambient temperature is in degrees Fahrenheit.

The two most common mechanisms for failure leading to fire are as follows: First, the rupture of an air conditioning hose located in close proximity to a hot exhaust. In this example, the refrigerant and refrigerant oil are discharged onto the hot exhaust causing the oil to auto ignite or a large cloud of vaporous VOC's that are ignited by a spark such as from the alternator or other source.

As noted above, the R-1234yf refrigerant is mildly flammable. Should a refrigerant line rupture with an ignition source present, then the refrigerant will accelerate the flaming combustion as well as the flaming spits of refrigerant oil.

The second most common example is when a battery positive cable has chafed on an air conditioning line. Air conditioning metal pipes and hoses are all grounded by virtue of being affixed to the engine and body. If a battery positive cable chafes against the line or hose to the point of creating a short-to-ground, this results in the battery cable arcing a hole in the line. There will be electrical arcing present as the refrigerant oil is spewed out as pressurized droplets. This failure mode will typically create a flaming cloud of spewing refrigerant oil droplets over the nearby components. Fire propagation depends on the potential of nearby components and combustibles.

PAG and mineral-based refrigerant oils will commonly auto ignite at temperatures of 500°F+. Full synthetic oils will auto ignite at temperatures of 800°F+. An electrical arc can generate localized spark temperatures in excess of several thousand degrees (2,000°F–4,000°F) at the failure site.[27]

Electrical failure mode is not limited to a chafed battery positive cable. Wiring nearby an air conditioning pipe can fail or an electric condenser fan can fail. Either failure mode can result in a ruptured AC line with electrical sparking or heat as the ignition source.

Other failure issues are that an air conditioning system can explode in a fire causing a sudden discharge of refrigerant and refrigerant oil into the flaming combustion. The escaping refrigerant oil will accelerate and help propagate the fire localized to the first breach in the system. Possibly, an unlawful refrigerant has been introduced into the system. As noted, some refrigerants are flammable. This author has observed common propane found in an air conditioning system.

The investigating engineer should establish what type of refrigerant and refrigerant oil were being used in the system for the vehicle being examined. If electrical shorting is suspected, the investigating tip is to inspect the wiring in question back at the lab. If the wire shorted to an aluminum line, there will be spatters of melted aluminum embedded in the cable at the arc site or where it shows signs of electrical activity. If present, this will establish the failure mode. A confounding factor in this analysis is if the front hood is constructed from aluminum. Generally, these type hoods will melt allowing melted bits of aluminum to flow down onto the other underhood components.

The critical analysis path here is proper identification of refrigerant oil used and correct diagnosis of primary failed part leading to fire. Due to the propensity of aluminum air conditioning components to be melted in an engine compartment fire, many times the fire evidence recovered is of poor quality.

E. Conclusion

In concluding this part of the analysis, the investigating engineer should understand that the greatest potential for a large order fire is for a flammable or combustible liquid to come into contact with a hot exhaust or some form of piloted ignition. Gasoline has the greatest BTU release potential per pound. Hence, over the years fuel system integrity designs have become much stronger. Additionally, the ability of the OBD II system to deliver any significant quantity of fuel to a leaking engine fuel rail after engine shut down is now severely limited.

The best way for an engineer to gain experience in the auto ignition and thermal transfer abilities of the different on-board flammable liquids, is to perform testing personally. The experiment to conduct an auto ignition test should be performed in a safe area. Using a gas burner with a protected supply hose, a piece of steel plate, and a pyrometer, a test jig can be easily constructed. When the steel has reached approximate similar operating temperatures as a typical exhaust system, expose the surface to varying quantities of the different flammable liquids. Proper safety clothing and eye protection is highly recommended. Varying the temperatures and quantities of flammable liquid used in these tests will yield data from which auto ignition temperature ranges can be reliably established and actual flames viewed personally.

3.3 Electrical Systems and Fire

Basic electricity: Think of DC electricity as water pressure in a pipe. The water pressure creates a force that can be used to perform work. Electricity is merely an exchange of electrons between molecules. This exchange of electrons can also be used to perform work. However, electricity flows around the conductor not through it as water does through a pipe.

Early electrical systems on domestic vehicles were 6-volt. Domestic vehicles switched from 6 to 12 volt systems starting around 1955. Import vehicles continued use of the 6-volt system through U.S. model year 1967. All modern vehicles sold on the U.S. market are currently 12-volt systems. As of the date of this writing, there are only tentative plans to implement the 42-volt system in automobiles. Manufacturers are anticipating an increase in demand by consumers for electric accessories and telematics. Further, by converting belt driven accessories such as power steering and air conditioning compressors over to electric motor driven units, there will be an increase in fuel economy.

Electrical component or wiring failures have historically been the source of the greatest number of automotive fires. Notably, electrical fire is generally the most limited type of electrical fire. There are a few instances where a major fire is the result of an electrical source. These is discussed in section 3.3.L, *High current flow computer modules.*

An electrical fire can range anywhere from a melted wire to actual flames erupting. The current definition used by NHTSA is that an electrical fire has occurred whenever a circuit's design has failed resulting in electrical heat sufficient to consume the immediate insulation.

All vehicles sold in the U.S. market must have "emergency" circuits. These circuits must operate regardless of the position of the ignition key. The emergency circuits are low and high beam headlamps, tail lamps, emergency four-way flashers, brake lamps, and horn.

Other circuits that operate without ignition key input are cabin lights, door warning lights, trunk lights, electric locks, electric seats, memory seats and mirrors, etc. These are commonly called "courtesy" circuits.

Small electrical fire is one area of analysis that is often misunderstood. Any investigator can only respond to his or her level of training and experience. Unless the fire investigator has an extensive work history in the automotive service industry, then his or her experience in actual vehicle electrical failures is limited to fires that required the services of the fire department.

Figure 3.5

Many vehicles that suffer an electrical failure that would qualify as a fire per the NHTSA definition are repairable. The vehicle is merely towed to a repair shop, fixed, then released back into service. Neither the fire investigator nor the investigating engineer will have observed these types of fire events to any significant degree.

Figures 3.5 and 3.6 depict a failed electric window switch on the left door panel of a 1999 Ford Explorer. The fire occurred while the vehicle was parked.

To understand any design issues, the investigating engineer should have a basic understanding of direct current (DC) electricity. Alternating current (AC) is also present in the alternator circuit. However, AC is rectified into DC via the internal "diode bridge" inside the alternator. Most of the electrical devices on an automobile currently operate on DC electricity. All circuit designs are subject to Ohm's law.

Ohm's law states that "the rate of the flow of the current is equal to electromotive force divided by resistance."[24,27]

The calculations for determining the different values for electrical properties in a circuit is easily explained in Figure 3.7. Ohm's law allows the engineer to calculate different values in a circuit when some of the electrical properties are known.

Figure 3.6

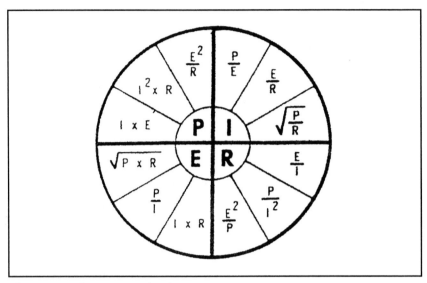

Figure 3.7 *Ohm's Law Wheel*

The four basic Ohm's law formulas are

$$I = E / R \quad R = E / I \quad E = I \times R \quad P = E \times I$$

where
I = intensity of current (amperes)
E = electromotive force (volts)
R = resistance (ohms)
P = power (watts)

The different calculations for arriving at circuit values using Ohm's law will be used when there is a design defect suspected. Typically, a design defect begins to present itself when there is greater than a 2-percent failure rate of a given component population. The failure may not necessarily have created a fire.

Many times a design defect will start out as a marginally designed circuit. If the design engineer did not leave sufficient redundancy in his or her design, then failure may result after the vehicle has been in service for a sufficient period of time for any heat deterioration or micro-corrosion to occur.

For example, the design engineer utilizes a field effect transistor to turn on the air conditioning clutch from the automatic air computer. When the vehicle left the factory the air gap at the clutch was smaller and the wiring loom had not been subjected to any oxidizing factors to cause micro-corrosion. After several months and many thousands of miles, the air gap at the air conditioning clutch has grown wider from age and usage. The circuit has also picked up 100 ohms of resistance from heat deterioration and micro-corrosion. The field effect transistor now determines that greater resistance exists in the circuit and will not flow the required amperage to engage the air conditioning clutch. The circuit has now failed because the design engineer did not allow sufficient redundancy in the circuit design to compensate for age and oxidation. A simple design change of increasing the cross sectional area or AWG size of the wire used would have avoided this design defect. As noted above, the trend is for design engineers to utilize bare minimum wire sizes to save on weight.

The greatest cause for an electrical meltdown in a circuit is for resistance to increase due to some causal factor. This causes less voltage to be present in the circuit. The battery attempts to compensate by increasing the available amperage. This in turn causes the circuit to heat up. If sufficient heat is allowed to build up then a meltdown and possible fire are the result. As a general rule, the older a circuit is the greater the resistance becomes over time. Resistance will further increase as a circuit heats up.

Circuit deterioration over time is a subject most automotive technicians are quite familiar with. Intermittent electrical failure issues are common. The connectors used in automotive, heavy truck and equipment all have male and female counterparts. Most connectors have multiple pins. Underhood connectors are commonly fitted with a rubber seal. Silicone grease is also utilized as a weatherproofing measure.

The female connector half is a press-fit onto the surface of the corresponding male pin. Over time—with vibration, heat, and weather—the integrity of the connector can become compromised. The grip of the female connector on the male counterpart can loosen or micro-corrosion can begin to form.

Another factor could be that too much current was being drawn through the affected male/female connector. This heats the female half connector, causing it to further loosen over time.

Weather ingress will cause micro-corrosion. If the vehicle is operated in snow country where the roads are salted, the corrosion will be worse. Micro-corrosion can also be an issue in flood vehicles. However, it takes many months to years for this type of corrosion to form. Sometimes, dielectric silicone grease will be found on connectors as a weatherproofing measure as OEM protection, or it was added by a technician when that connector was serviced.

Deteriorating contacts inside relays can increase circuit resistance. This can cause heat deterioration in a connector over time.

Regardless of how they come to be, bad connection can and do happen. Simply put, a dead short will blow the fuse unless the circuit has no fuse protection.

A bad connection can cause an electrical fire. As a general rule, the deterioration of a circuit leading to a fire occurs over time.

The following is a list of electrical and electromechanical devices which are capable of causing an operational mode fire:

- battery
- alternator
- starter motor
- HVAC blower motor/electric motors
- engine ignition coil
- electrical switches
- solenoids
- wiring looms
- fuse and relay panel
- headlamps
- electric seat track or seat heater
- high-current flow computer modules

A. Battery fire

In simplified terms, think of a battery as a sponge held between two slats. Dip the sponge and slats into a bucket of water. The water will represent the electrolyte. Squeeze the slats and our "battery" runs out of water and requires recharging. Over repeated cycles, the sponge begins to tatter and fray. It will no longer accept or transfer as much water as it did when it was new. Eventually, the sponge is so frayed that it will no longer absorb or transfer water. This same decline will occur in all types of batteries. All batteries will deteriorate over time and duty use cycles.

Essentially, a battery is a device that uses chemical energy to create electrical energy. A battery consists of two dissimilar metals each isolated from the other. These are termed "anode" for the negative plate and "cathode" for the positive plate. Both the battery positive and negative plates will be immersed in either a caustic acid or alkali solution called an "electrolyte." The battery plates will touch the electrolyte but are kept separate from each other by an insulator. The electrolyte is similar to a "stew" containing molecules with positively charged electrons called "cations" and negatively charged electrons called "anions."

When the circuit is turned on, the anion electrons will migrate up the negative plates. This creates the voltage present in the circuit. At the same time, the cation electrons will migrate up the positive plates. The cation electrons are the electromotive force (amperage) in the circuit. Amperage is the element in electricity that provides the power in the circuit to turn a motor, light a lamp, etc. The voltage must be present in the circuit for the amperage to flow. As the voltage available in the circuit drops, the battery will allow the current to increase in an effort to keep the circuit running.

The end result is either the battery will give up electrons until it is dead or the circuit will overheat causing some type of failure up to and including fire potential. A higher current flow in the circuit will increase the potential for electrical failure leading to fire.

A battery fire is caused by a short in the primary (+) side to the ground (–) side or by a high resistance connection. Battery cables will typically connect to the starter motor with an AWG wire size of "0" to "0000." There will be a second connection to the Power Distribution Module or fusible links. These wires will typically be an AWG size of #8 to #10. The Power Distribution Module is a fuse and relay box typically found under the hood. Most vehicles have one. However, there are some high-line vehicles that have two and three Power Distribution Modules.

Wire and cable size will determine how much current flow that a given circuit is capable of handling without overheating the circuit. The U.S. market and the SAE refer to the American Wire Gauge (AWG) system for vehicles sold in the U.S. In European and Asian vehicles, the wire diameter is referred to as "cross sectional area" (CSA).

Table 3.1
Wire and Cable Specifications and Applications Chart[25]

	Number and Diameter of Strands	Nominal CSA of Core	Nominal Outside Diameter	Resistance per Meter at 20°C (Ohms)	Approximate Continuous Current Rating	Equivalent American Gauge	Typical Application
General Purpose Cables	9/0.30	0.65	2.35	0.0294	5.75	18	dash, side, tail
	14/0.30	1.0	2.55	0.0189	8.75	16	accessories
	21/0.30	1.5	2.85	0.0125	12.75	14-16	accessories and
	28/0.30	2.0	3.15	0.0094	17.50	14	headlamps
	35/0.30	2.5	3.55	0.0075	21.75	12-14	ammeter and
	44/0.30	3.0	3.95	0.0080	25.50	12	battery feed
	56/0.30	4.0	4.25	0.00471	32.00	10	battery and
	65/0.30	4.5	4.85	0.0041	35.00	10	alternator
	84/0.30	6.0	5.70	0.0031	42.00	8	circuits
	97/0	7.0	6.00	0.0027	50.00	8	HD alternator
	120/0.30	8.5	6.80	0.0022	60.00	8	deep cycle battery circuit
Starter Cables	37/0.71	15.0	7.75	0.0011	105.00	0	starter circuits
	266/0.30	20.0	9.20	0.0010	135.00	00	
	37/0.90	25.0	9.40	0.0006	170.00	000	
	61/0.90	40.0	11.45	0.0005	300.00	0000	
	61/1/.13	60.0	13.75	0.0003	415.00	00000	

A given size of wire is capable of sustaining current spikes beyond its normal rating for short periods of time. Generally, a given circuit wire size will tolerate approximately 30 percent greater current draw than it is rated for quite a period of time before the circuit begins to heat up. However, pyrolysis of the insulation will eventually develop, causing the insulation to crack and break down.

The factors which cause DC circuits to heat up are high resistance in a positive section, a high resistance short-to-ground, or a very poor connection. If a positive battery lead develops a significant contact with ground, then this causes the battery circuit to overheat and produce hydrogen gasses. The circuit either heats up to point of ignition or a spark occurs. This causes the battery to explode shattering the battery casing. Sometimes, the battery lug post will shrink inside the battery cable clamp when too much amperage is drawn through the lug.

Table 3.1 lists the equivalent AWG and CSA sizes, the current carrying capacity of the different sizes, and typical application of different wire sizes.

There are four primary performance rating systems for automotive batteries sold in the U.S. market:

- **cranking performance** also referred to as "cold cranking amps": This method will state a figure such as "625 CCA." This means that the battery is capable of sustaining 625 amps at 0°F (–18°C) while still maintaining a voltage across the terminals of not less than 7.2 volts.
- **reserve capacity**. The reserve capacity is listed in minutes such as 39–86–100 or longer. It is a measurement of the length of time a 12-volt battery can deliver 25 amps while still maintaining a terminal voltage of at least 10.2 volts at a temperature of 80°F (27°C).
- **ampere-hour**. This method rates a battery capacity based on a 20-hour rate. This represents the steady current a battery can deliver for 20 hours at a temperature of 80°F (27°C) without terminal voltage dropping below 10.5 volts for a 12-volt battery.
- **watts**. This method is a measurement of battery cranking power available at 0°F (–18°C) to crank an engine over. Amperes are units of measure of the amount of current flowing in a closed circuit, and voltage is the electrical pressure or force applied to the circuit. Multiplying volts by amps will give the watts available in the circuit.

Regardless of which type of rating system used, there is one underlying fact which affects all automotive batteries: a battery is a poor way to store energy.

For example, compare the energy available from one gallon of gasoline to the number of batteries it takes to produce the same amount of BTUs. Where:

One gallon of gasoline contains 150,000 BTUs/hr (average)
One fully charged automotive battery rated at 3,750 watts (625 CCA)
To convert BTUs/hr to watts the multiplier is 0.2931.[30]

150,000 × 0.2931 = 43,965 watts
43,965 / 3,750 = 11.7 automotive batteries

Thus, it takes almost a total of twelve batteries to equal the same BTUs contained in one gallon of gas. However, it should be noted that the BTU release rate for gasoline is exponentially faster than DC current is capable of creating. Electrical heat release is slow in nature.

Another factor to consider is the ability of electrical heat to conduct or communicate itself to other parts compared to the ability of flaming gasoline to conduct heat. Gasoline has a clear advantage because good mechanical contact is required for electrical heat.

When a lead-acid battery has the electrolyte added to the cells, it is much like being born. The electrolyte acid forms a chemical reaction to the lead, antimony, and cadmium in the battery plates and the plates begin to produce polarized electrical molecules which travel up the grid plate to be collected at the terminals for use. Please note the chemical reaction will produce some electrical presence. However, the battery must be charged.

Whether a battery is fully charged and used or sits on a shelf, this process causes a whitish coating to begin forming on the plates called "sulfiding." The process of lead sulfiding will occur at a known rate. If the battery charge is allowed to discharge, the lower voltage will accelerate the sulfiding deterioration of the plates. Thus, a battery has the greatest amount of heat energy available when new and in a fully charged state. The available electrical charge the battery can deliver diminishes with age until the battery can no longer start the engine and cannot be recharged.

As noted above, when a battery is being charged or in a state of high discharge there will be the production of hydrogen gasses emitted from the vents. These gasses are explosive. A charged battery which has suffered a significant dead short will commonly explode. Many times there will be an arc bead in the battery cable at the point of failure or melted or shrunken battery posts. Please note that the presence of an arc bead does not necessarily indicate this was the area of origin of the fire.[27]

In the case of multiple battery applications, there will typically be an isolation solenoid or isolation transformer which separates the battery positive cables when the engine is not operating. This allows the driver to utilize accessories until the cabin battery goes dead and still start the engine. Both batteries are con-

Figure 3.8

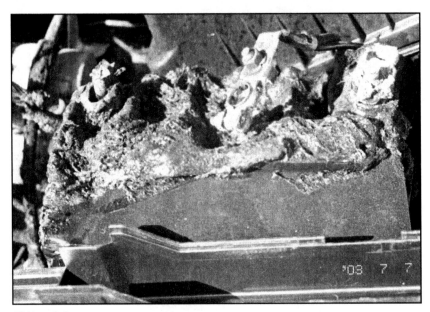

Figure 3.9

nected to the alternator positive terminal to recharge. The isolation solenoid or transformer will automatically disconnect when the key is in the off or accessory position. Figures 3.8 and 3.9 depict a 2001 Toyota Camry battery fire.

B. Alternator fires

The alternator or generator will recharge the battery as the engine operates. There are two main differences between an alternator and a generator. The difference is that an alternator produces alternating current (AC) which must be rectified to direct current (DC) so that the battery can charge and the rest of the accessories will work. The second difference is that an alternator produces electricity from its field windings where a generator produces electricity from its armature. Generators began disappearing from domestic vehicles in the late 1950s. Import vehicles used generators through 1969. All modern vehicles are now equipped with alternators.

Most alternators are geared for the vehicle's anticipated consumption of current by the consumer. A standard design parameter is for the alternator to meet or barely exceed the total "peak" consumption of all the accessories. Any design of alternator should not be run with an average demand which is greater than 70–75 percent of its rated capacity.

For example, a hypothetical vehicle has a maximum consumption requirement of 60 amps average with all accessories on during operation. An alternator with a rated capacity of approximately 85 amps should be equipped. This unit will produce 60 amps on a continuous basis without overheating (in theory). Most alternator designs in this class will also be capable of short spikes of demand up to 100+ amps without damage to the alternator. However, if that same alternator is operated in a circuit that continuously demands greater than 100 amps, then the alternator will heat up and eventually fail, possibly causing a fire.

There are four principal styles of alternator design being used on all model vehicles and heavy trucks sold in the U.S. market. These are the compact claw-pole, the windingless rotor, the salient-pole, and the compact liquid cooled. The investigating engineer should refer to the proper workshop manual for current rating and proper identification of any suspected alternator.

As an alternator or generator operates, it generates heat normally. Most alternators are air cooled, although some designs of alternators will utilize a coolant line from the engine coolant to cool the housing. Some alternators will produce single-phase AC electricity (before rectification). Some alternators will produce three-phase AC electricity.

The diode bridge is an integral part of all alternators. It has two functions: First, it functions to rectify the alternating current into direct current. Second, it prevents reverse current from the battery entering the alternator through the field windings to ground when the alternator is not rotating. If reverse current were allowed through the field windings, this would cause the wiring to overheat, possibly causing a fire.

A diode is an electronic device in an electronic circuit that allows current to flow in only one direction. It works something like a one-way valve. Diodes have been known to "leak" and allow some current flow in the opposite direction than what is desired. Diodes do not always fail in a fully open or fully shorted state. When positive electrons become present in the negative portion of the diode, failure of that diode is typically not far behind. A weak diode will many times cause the entire diode bridge to fail.

The voltage regulator is located outside the alternator housing on early alternator systems. Almost all modern alternator designs incorporate the voltage regulator into the alternator housing. Essentially, this component measures the amount of voltage flowing in a circuit, then adjusts the output of the alternator according to the needs of the electrical system. As a battery reaches full charge, the voltage regulator will cut back on alternator output.

The question the investigating engineer must answer when inspecting an electrical fire that appears to have originated in the alternator area is whether or not the alternator was the cause or a victim of the fire. A second issue the investigating engineer should address is whether or not the vehicle battery was shorted internally. A badly shorted battery can cause the alternator to burn out. As noted previously, the sulfiding process reduces the capacity of any automotive battery. The shorted cell(s) can cause damage to the diode bridge.

Generally, when an alternator begins to fail from overheating there will be internal signs. The alternator will require disassembly first. The areas to inspect are the front and rear bearing or bushing. Bearing damage indicators are a seized bearing, a rough rotational feel, visible damage such as a crack or worn valley, and physical scraping of the field coils by the armature. As an alternator overheats, many times the unit will sling solder from the armature windings all over the inside of the casing.

The next area of the alternator the investigating engineer should inspect is the battery positive (+) connection. The two most common designs are a push on connector and a nut with a ring lug on the wire. Strong and clean mechanical connection is required regardless of the design used. As alternators increase in capacity, the battery lug will also increase in size. For alternators with a threaded rear lug, a design capacity of less than 100 amps will use a 1/4" (6 mm) bolt. For alternators above 100 amps the lug size increases to 5/16" (8 mm).

Many times the diode bridge inside the alternator will have a diode which begins to leak or break down internally. This causes a condition known as "ripple volts." Ripple voltage occurs when the AC waveform or negative is allowed to enter the DC section, or when negative electrons are entering the positive area. This will cause alternator overheating. This condition is sometimes manifested by a dimly glowing "charge" lamp icon on the dashboard. Interestingly, the battery seems to charge normally when this condition occurs. A "hard" failure of the diode bridge, windings, or other components will cause the alternator to not work at all with the "charge" lamp fully illuminated. The investigating engineer should question the driver of the vehicle being examined to find out if such a condition with the charge indicator lamp had been observed in the days or weeks prior to the failure.

Another type of fire that can occur from an alternator is if the diode bridge is allowing some reverse current through the field windings while the vehicle is parked and the engine is off. This condition can also occur while an alternator is under operation. The windings and alternator housing will typically show signs of overheating from internal electrical heat. Essentially, the field windings are nothing more than a rather long path to ground. The electrical heat will generally manifest itself in more than one winding. There may be melting at the heat sink around the diode bridge, voltage regulator area, alternator casing, and/or alternator bracket.

Figure 3.10 *Alternator fire.*

Figure 3.11 *Alternator fire.*

Many designs of alternators will use a "fusible link" for the battery positive cable. All or part of the battery positive cable that goes from the alternator to the battery positive lug is designed to melt away. A fusible link will typically be comprised of a high tin alloy in the cable. Tin melts at a considerably lower temperature than copper. However, a fusible link will not always prevent an alternator fire from a failing diode bridge. The investigating engineer should be sure to check the OEM specifications for the alternator and alternator cable to determine design type and materials the unit is comprised from. Figures 3.10 and 3.11 depict a failed alternator that led to an engine fire.

If the investigation indicates recent replacement of or work on the alternator, this introduces the issue of non-OEM parts being utilized in the overhaul of the alternator. It also raises the possibility that the battery primary circuit was damaged or not properly inspected by the repair shop. The investigating engineer should examine all phases of the repair.

Automotive repair industry standards for alternator replacement hold that a technician should first check the capacity of the battery to take and hold a charge. The battery should be checked first. Both of the battery terminals should be thoroughly cleaned and electrolyte checked (non-maintenance free type). If battery charge is low, it should be charged up and load tested before the replacement alternator is tested on the engine. A battery that has a significant internal short can damage the alternator.

Next, the technician should next use a digital voltmeter to perform a "voltage drop" test. All portions of underhood battery positive cables should be tested including alternator, starter, and Power Distribution Module. If the reading is greater than 0.2 volts, then an issue within the battery primary circuit exists. Finally, a conventional carbon pile load tester should be used to ensure the alternator actual output is within 10 percent of rated output. The alternator output test is performed with the engine running at or above 1,500–1,800 rpm. Please note some manufacturers will allow 0.5 volts as the danger threshold for feedback or ripple voltage.

The voltage drop test consists of attaching the digital voltmeter positive lead to battery positive. The negative lead from the meter is touched to the B+ terminal of the alternator, then to the positive lug on the starter, and finally to the positive lug on the Power Distribution Module. Thus, the meter is connected to both ends of the positive cable but *not* to ground. If a reading occurs, this means that negatively charged electrons are present in the positive side of the circuit. This is an undesirable condition. The source of the negative ripple voltage must be found and repaired.

It is also usual and customary practice in the auto repair industry for the technician to physically check the battery positive cables for signs of chafing or insulation breakdown, to clean all terminals in the charging and starter circuits, load test the battery and load test the replacement alternator after installation.

If the B+ cable to the alternator were chafed to the point the circuit was suffering excessive ripple voltage, then this could be why the alternator failed in the first place. The replacement alternator may fail also. However, the greatest danger is from the chafed insulation creating a fire hazard. This is why technicians engage in the practice of checking the battery positive cable for insulation damage and load testing the output of the replacement alternator.

If the alternator passes the voltage drop test and a load test, this greatly reduces the chance of failure leading to fire shortly after the repaired vehicle leaves the auto shop.

Finally, it is usual and customary for a technician to perform a "parasitic draw" test when a vehicle is brought in for service with a history of battery failure issues. The parasitic draw test will isolate which part(s) of the circuits are staying on or are drawing current from the battery when the vehicle is off and parked. As a general rule, any parasitic draw greater than 45 milliamps will lead to battery failure over time. Notably, if the affected vehicle is driven rarely or driven only short distances repeatedly without any long trips, then an excessive parasitic draw condition will present sooner than a vehicle that is driven 50+ miles each day in one single trip.

C. Starter motor fires

A starter motor is one of the heaviest single draw components on a vehicle. It functions for only a few seconds. Either the engine starts and the starter resumes a rest position or the engine does not start and the starter motor continues to be turned over by the driver until the battery runs dead.

A starter motor is either a series wound, shunt wound, or permanent magnet energized DC motor. All motors are nothing more than a dead short to the electrical system until the armature begins to rotate. As the ignition switch first engages the starter, a high electrical spike results in the system. After the spike in the system, the amperage draw will drop down to normal draw. This is referred to as "peak" and "continuous" draw. Just like all other electrical motors, the older the unit becomes, the greater the internal friction becomes. The armature becomes increasingly difficult to rotate with age. This can cause the electrical system to heat up and eventually catch fire.

A starter fire can result by continued cranking of the starter motor or by an old starter motor. As an electrical circuit begins to lose voltage presence, the amperage begins to increase. This generates electrical heat resulting in eventual circuit meltdown.

Should a starter ever catch fire, the fire will be limited to the battery cables and possibly the starter solenoid. The starter solenoid is essentially a relay which allows large amounts of current to be conducted using a small wire to the ignition switch as the control wire. It also physically moves the starter drive gear outward to mesh with the engine flywheel. The ability of the fire to spread depends on the availability of a nearby secondary fuel. This will be discussed in greater detail in Section 3.5.

D. HVAC and other electric motor fire

The HVAC blower motor is a conventional parallel wound DC motor. The speeds for the motor are controlled either through the use of a series resistor or a computer in the case of automatic climate control systems.

The greatest failure in all electric motors is the propensity to heat up the circuit as the friction on the armature increases with wear. If enough drag on the armature occurs then a circuit meltdown is imminent. Essentially, an electric motor is nothing more than a dead short until the armature begins to rotate. If an ammeter is connected into any circuit with an electric motor and the motor is switched on, the ammeter will first spike high (peak watts) then drop to the load normal for that motor (continuous watts).

With computer-controlled "automatic air" systems, the HVAC computer controller in the dash can fail internally leading to fire. Most of the systems are a digital control panel operating analog circuits. The analog circuits contain sufficient current to cause an electrical fire.

The critical analysis path for the investigating engineer here is key to the wording of FMVSS 302. As discussed, the code requires that any component within 13 mm of the passenger airspace be compliant with the code. Manufacturers will separate the passenger air space from the HVAC ducting by a trim panel. This allows the manufacturer to utilize a more cost-effective composite on the HVAC ducting. Unfortunately, the more cost-effective composites are generally more combustible.

E. Engine ignition coil

The engine ignition coil is present on all engines. On most modern designs, the distributor has been eliminated in favor of computer-controlled multi-coil systems mounted one on each spark plug. The latter coil systems is commonly called "coil-over" ignition coils.

Older ignition coils used with breaker point systems are generally oil cooled. These are standard inductive current coils. These units are comprised of thousands of wraps of wire around an iron core. The wire originates at the positive terminal and terminates at the negative terminal or core. Most of these early systems will produce 18,000–20,000 volts at the center tap when the field is collapsed. The coils are cooled by an oil-based compound.

Later designs use the same type of design with the exception of many more layers of wire wrapped around the iron core. These designs will produce 45,000–60,000 volts. An epoxy is used to seal the wiring. Oil is no longer used to cool the coils. The coils are air-cooled. The newer multicoil systems will have a computerized driver generally located under the dashboard, separate from the coils, or mounted on the tops of the sparkplugs incorporated into the spark coil units. This computer may be combined with the engine management system or it may be a standalone. The investigating engineer will need to refer to the workshop manual for the vehicle being inspected to resolve this issue.

The older style of an oil-filled coil is more combustible than the modern coil-over type constructed from epoxy. A coil-over design will have one coil per spark plug. The spark plug boot is part of the coil assembly. The assembly is pushed down over the spark plug then bolted to the engine. In this configuration, each spark plug has its own coil. There is no distributor as with conventional coils.

As the spark plugs age, creating a larger air gap, or if the circuit picks up resistance, this can allow the circuit to heat up. Damage can manifest itself as wiring insulation burn-back at the spark plug wires or at the positive connection itself. On modern vehicles it is possible for the ignition control module to also

Figure 3.12

Figure 3.13

heat up and ignite the wiring insulation from excessive resistance on the spark plug multi-coils. Figures 3.12 and 3.13 depict a burned ignition coil driver module on a 1999 VW Jetta.

The critical analysis path here is for the investigating engineer to understand that the computers, wiring, and dash cluster can be exempt from FMVSS 302. Only the outer plastic cover of the instrument cluster is required to be code compliant due to its proximity to the air space of the passenger area. Unless a component is located directly within 13 mm of passenger air space it may be constructed from more flammable plastics. However, as a general rule automobile manufacturers will utilize compliant composites throughout the interior on modern vehicles.

F. Electrical switch fire

Switches are electromechanical devices. There are two operational failure modes. The first type of switch failure mode is a switch that becomes overheated due to too much current flow in the circuit. The switch heats up and melts internally. Some examples of these types of switches are the headlamps, the ignition switch, and electric window switches.

The second type of switch failure mode is for switches to ground internally. The most susceptible is the polarity-reversing switch. These types of switches are generally found in older electric window or sunroof circuits. Since the motor being controlled must rotate in both directions, the switch must be able to switch polarity internally. If the switch malfunctions where the positive is allowed to cross with the negative, the switch will heat up and melt internally. On some circuits, this may happen when the key is off. The OEM workshop manual contains the correct electrical system schematic for the vehicle being examined.

G. Solenoids

Some types of solenoids are designed for continuous duty. The propensity for this type of solenoid to cause an electrical fire is fairly low. Momentary duty solenoids such as those found in electric door locks will not tolerate a continuous duty cycle. The danger of heat buildup happens when the lock mechanism sticks, the lock relay sticks, or an alarm system lock function causes the solenoid to stick on. The coil windings heat up, eventually melting and possibly catching fire.

The critical analysis tip for the investigating engineer here is to determine if the door or dashboard burned from the inside-out or vice-versa. The wiring and the mechanical device being controlled by the solenoid should be inspected to determine if the circuit shows any signs of heat being generated from the solenoid sticking on.

H. Wiring looms

The main problem with wiring looms is that, as wire ages, the loom will pick up resistance that was not there when it was new. Another factor is that resistance increases in relation to the increasing amount of heat it is exposed to. As discussed in Section 3.3, oxidation of the connectors, conductor, and insulation will occur over time, as well as with exposure to severe service environments such as road salt or desert heat. Another issue affecting wiring looms is that parts of the loom may be located under or near the battery. During normal use, the battery outgasses corrosive vapors that are heavier than air. If the wiring loom, power connector, or Power Distribution Module are located in close proximity, accelerated corrosion leading to failure is a common issue.

Again, this degradation issue will be readily recognized by master technicians and field service engineers that work for automobile manufacturers or have worked in the automotive service industry for many years. However, if the investigating engineer or fire investigator does not have a work history in the automotive service industry, his or her experience with these issues will be limited to non-existent.

The insulation on automotive wire is not required to have any more heat, moisture, or oil ingress protection than house wiring. The most common type of insulation is comprised of polyvinyl chloride or polyethylene over stranded wire. The wire itself is protected by convolute conduit (crinkle tube) and black PVC electrical tape. This provides the manufacturers with flexibility to bend the wire into tight places. Unfortunately, these are the most combustible of the plastic insulating materials. However, transfer temperatures will be low. The principal difference is if the convolute conduit is comprised of thermoplastics or thermoset plastics. No standard is specified by NHTSA. Fire testing from an exemplar vehicle may be the only means of gathering data on the convolute conduit used on that particular year, make, and model.

A building engineer or CFI that handles only structure fires will typically not see how electrical heat affects stranded wire. Buildings will not typically incorporate stranded wire in the main electrical circuits feeding the outlets. Solid core wire or Romex® is commonly the wire of choice. Stranded wire failures have a different appearance than those found in solid core wire.

Corporate Average Fuel Economy (CAFE) regulations is another design factor for the investigating engineer to consider. The current vehicle designs are moving toward using lighter components to meet the increasing requirements for better gas mileage.

Wiring looms can weigh up to 90 pounds. This is one of the areas lightened up to minimal margins. The electrical engineering department will typically select the absolute minimal wire diameter to handle the anticipated current draw.

Figure 3.14

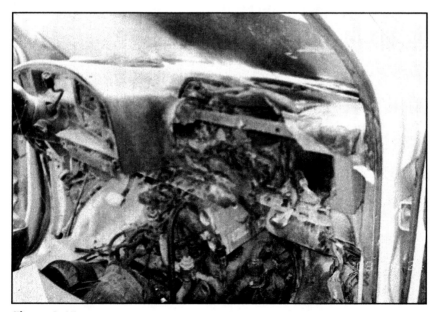

Figure 3.15

This approach does not allow sufficient redundancy in the circuit for the increase in resistance which occurs normally with age and high mileage. The wire in the circuit could heat up to the melting point for the insulation, causing auto ignition.

Should the wiring loom be in close vicinity of a secondary fuel source such as a fuel line, brake fluid reservoir, instrument cluster or HVAC ducting, then this may promote a greater consumption of the vehicle composites.

Figures 3.14 and 3.15 depict a wiring loom failure which caused this dash fire on a 1993 Ford Econoline van. The engine side of the firewall showed minimal heat damage with the hood up. However, there is heavy consumption of the dashboard composites on the passenger compartment side of the firewall.

The connectors on the ends of the individual legs of the wiring loom can cause electrical heat. The connector may develop a high resistance condition due to poor mechanical conductivity of one of the crimps or micro-corrosion. The heat will build up, eventually melting the connector, with the potential for fire. Vibration causing looseness in the connector and moisture ingress are also common service failure issues. Many manufacturers will incorporate a weatherproofing measure by use of silicone grease at each connector exposed to weather.

Most modern vehicles sold in the U.S. market are compliant with the DIN Standard Number 72552-Terminal Designation Numbering.[10] This standard establishes an industry recommended practice of numbering common circuit connections the same on all vehicles sold. Almost every relay terminal, ignition coil terminal, and switch terminal will have a small number cast into the plastic next

Table 3.2
Connector Identification Chart[10]

Terminal Number	Terminal Definition
1	Negative side of ignition coil
15	Ignition positive
15a	Ballast resistor to ignition positive
30	Battery positive feed wire from or to ignition
31	Battery ground feed wire
45	Starter or inhibit relay
54	Brake lamps
56	Head lamps
58	Side marker and tail lamps
B+	Battery positive
B-	Battery ground
D+	Generator positive

to the terminal to indicate its purpose. Understanding the basic designations will assist the investigating engineer in determining the nature of the circuit in question while working in the field.

Table 3.2 shows some of the more commonly found designations of wiring connector numbers using DIN 72552 codes.

For example, the investigating engineer is analyzing a failed and melted circuit. The relay which powers the circuit has a terminal on its base labeled "30." This indicates that this relay has an unfused positive wire feeding this terminal which may or may not be controlled by the ignition switch. This identification of the wire as unfused positive may be germane to the diagnosis of the failure.

I. Power Distribution Module

Most modern vehicles have a fuse and relay panel also termed a Power Distribution Module. The vehicle being examined may have more than one Power Distribution Module. The investigator may also find computer modules located inside the Power Distribution Modules. Most vehicles also locate at least one separate fuse panel inside the vehicle.

The type and location of fuse and relay panels will vary widely for the different vehicle makes. There may be multiple relay locations at remote locations throughout the vehicle. Some modern vehicle designs will locate the relay inside the motorized assembly. Some examples of this are electric window motor and windshield wiper motor assemblies.

The best method for identifying the fuse or relay suspected of being the causal factor of an electrical fire is the workshop manual for that specific vehicle. However, this entails purchasing a separate manual for each model investigated. There is another method available from aftermarket publishers such as Mitchell® Manuals, Chiltons®, or Motors®. These publishers all offer a component locator guide. These are simple schematic pictures and architectural drawings of the actual component identified as it is located in the vehicle. Other options to locate technical information can be found on technical websites maintained by automobile manufacturers and aftermarket technical publishers. A one-day subscription can be purchased to allow access to research and download applicable technical information from the website regarding the vehicle being examined. The investigating engineer or CFI should procure the correct wiring schematic and component locator to review *before* the fire investigation is conducted. This will allow the investigator to have a general idea of the wiring and component layout in the vehicle before teardown is initiated.

As with all electrical systems, fuse and relay panels suffer deterioration at the connections and relay contacts. As circuits get older, these connections naturally loosen due to mechanical vibration. The normal arcing that occurs in relay

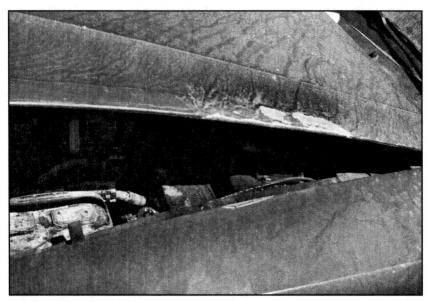

Figure 3.16 Power Distribution Module fire, 2006 Ford Mustang.

Figure 3.17 Power Distribution Module fire, 2006 Ford Mustang.

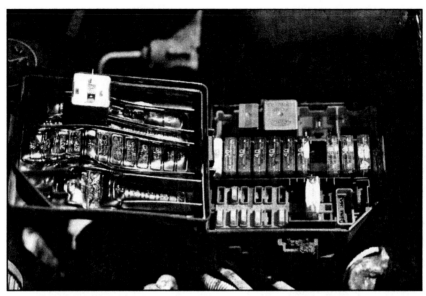

Figure 3.18 *Same 2006 Ford Mustang as seen in Figure 3.16.*

and solenoid contacts will also cause resistance in the circuit. The arcing may result in the heavy current contacts "welding" themselves together such that the relay cannot break the circuit. This condition generally leads to circuit meltdown. Figures 3.16 through 3.18 depict a failed Power Distribution Module that occurred to a 2006 Ford Mustang.

Another process of deterioration called "electrolysis" occurs when two dissimilar metals are brought together in the presence of electricity. This causes a crusty buildup which starts with micro-corrosion. Pitting on relay contacts can cause relays to stick or introduce resistance into a circuit. Many relay or contactor (high amperage relays or solenoids) surfaces that have high cyclical rates will commonly be coated with a hardened alloy of silver. This allows much more use of the relay or contactor before any pitting occurs. Regardless of the source, if a connection or relay contact builds sufficient heat to cause meltdown, then fire is a likely possibility.

Most modern manufacturers have utilized flame-retardant polymeric composites to comprise the actual plastic surrounding the fuse and relay panel. These higher flame-retardant plastics can also be found in the cowling surrounding the steering columns. Most modern vehicles sold on the U.S. market will identify these plastics per SAE J1344.

As noted previously, there is a much greater potential for electrical fire erupting in circuits that have developed high resistance. In most cases, a dead short to ground in a fused circuit is a more desirable type of failure than in a circuit where heat is allowed to build. The fuse or fusible link will snap, terminating electricity in the circuit in the dead short example, whereas the insulation will melt and possibly catch fire in an overheating circuit.

The critical analysis path for the investigating engineer to understand in analyzing a fuse panel or relay fire is to determine if the relay or relay panel is the cause or a victim of the fire, and which was the primary failed circuit.

First, the correct wiring schematic and component locator data should be procured so that the individual components and wiring can be identified as the investigation progresses. The affected area should de-layered carefully. The relay casings or relay housing should be separated using utmost caution. The purpose is to determine if the relay or relay panel melted from inside-outward or from outside-inward. The components should be analyzed to determine which portions show the greatest amount of heat. All fuses and fusible links should be checked at their blades or terminals to see if there were signs of electrical heat prior to failure. This will appear as a bluish hue or similar discoloration to the affected metal area of the connector blade or socket. There may be signs of heat in more than one circuit. It is characteristic of a DC circuit failure to show signs of overheating both at the area of failure in the circuit and at the source. The destruction of the insulation will then work its way to the center.

J. Headlamps

This type of fire is usually easily identified. Generally, the only damage is to the headlamp area itself. There may be some localized damage. However, most of the designs do not locate any components near the headlamps except the wire feed for the lamp itself.

There is a newer type of lamp used on modern vehicles called a "high intensity discharge" or "projector lamp." These units will utilize an argon or xenon gas to enhance brilliance. This analysis does not apply to the aftermarket halogen "cool blue" super-bright replacements for OEM halogen lamps. The projector lamp units can either be OEM or aftermarket add-ons. All of these units will have a computerized driver located near the lamp it powers. Typically, there will be one or two computerized drivers per headlamp. These units can build heat and cause a circuit meltdown. As noted above, these failures will typically be localized to the side it powers.

The biggest problem with headlamp circuits is that the headlamps will sit out and will be operated in the weather. Over a period of time, the weatherproofing measures taken by the factory may break down and allow moisture ingress. This results in a high resistance connection at the headlamp connector. Figures 3.19 and 3.20 depict a headlamp fire on a 2000 Honda Civic.

Figure 3.19

Figure 3.20

Another factor for the investigating engineer to check is if the headlamp housing has been modified or replaced with an aftermarket unit as collision repair. Young automotive enthusiasts will install aftermarket headlamp assemblies or possibly attach a replacement front cover over the OEM rear housing half. These plastics may not have the same non-combustible characteristics as the complete OEM unit.

K. Electric seat track or seat heaters

Electric seats have been equipped on domestic vehicles and imports sold in the U.S. market since the middle 1960s. At first, these options were found only on luxury vehicles. As time progressed, manufacturers found that the American consumer was willing to pay for these luxuries on midline vehicles also. Almost all modern midline vehicles sold today offer the electric seat track and seat heater as options. Most luxury vehicles have these as standard equipment. Some luxury vehicles offer "memory seats" which automatically adjust to preset locations by pressing a button.

As with all electric motors and electromechanical devices, if the motor armature or the mechanism jams, then the circuit will begin to heat up. Lubricated seat tracks become gummy with age. This causes the seat motor armature to drag. The same issue develops with the drive cables operated by the seat track motors to adjust the seat. Debris and dust from passenger operation accumulates in the track grooves. Normal tracking times for an electric seat from one end to the other is approximately 13–15 seconds. If the seat is moving slower than that, there may be some binding that can cause heat.

Another common failure which can result in circuit melting is that the main power feed for the seat motors can dislodge from the original anchoring and become pinched in the track or frame causing either high resistance or shorting to ground.

Seat heaters are a popular option in cold weather country. These units are a flexible mat layered into the upholstery. Most designs feature resistive wire in a specialized polypropylene or polyurethane covering. These units incorporate a thermistor to maintain a specified heat range.

It should be noted that most modern electric seat track designs use relays for operation. The switch is only designed for relay activation. Older models will use a more robust design which allows the switch to conduct the amperage to the motorized track. If the model uses memory seats, then the circuit will have a memory module located remotely from the seat. The electric seat feature will universally be connected to a primary wire which is electrified while the key is in the off position. Typically, features like "memory" seats will be found only on high-line vehicles.

There is a somewhat rare type of seat fire that can occur to modern vehicles that use a crash data recording system in the SRS (airbag) module. Check manufacturer specifications to determine if the vehicle being examined contains such a system. These systems contain an *accelerometer* (an electronic device that measures applied force) cast inside the seat foam of one or both front seats. The applied force signal sent from the accelerometer is recorded in the SRS crash data system for later retrieval. These data assist with accident reconstruction studies. Some seat designs incorporate a metal box that performs as an occupant sensor. Some systems will incorporate an "air bladder" with a switch that performs as an occupant sensor. Other seat designs will incorporate the actual side impact airbag module inside the seat frame. These designs are for thorax protection.

The failure can occur two ways: first, an electrical failure from wiring internal to the seat assembly. For example, the seatbelt switch circuit shorts or otherwise crosses into the accelerometer wiring. Second, the SRS module fails internally and sends too high a positive feed to the accelerometer or to the airbag module. The accelerometer or airbag module heats up and melts a hole in the seat. There may be some slight combustion of the seat foam and upholstery surrounding the hole. These types of fires usually snuff out from lack of ignition mechanism and production of NOx gasses. The interior of the vehicle will have

Figure 3.21 Ford clock spring fire.

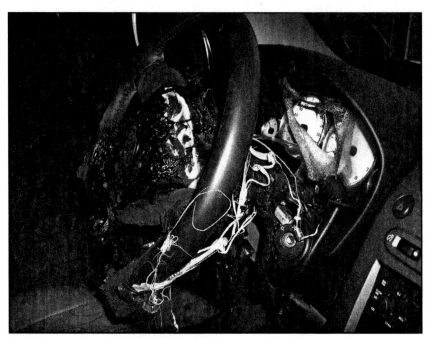

Figure 3.22 *Ford clock spring fire.*

suffered heavy smoke damage. This failure has been observed to occur in parked vehicles.

Sometimes SRS systems will fail internally allowing the airbag module to heat up resulting in a fire. This type of failure can also occur in the "clockspring" (rotary coupler) located behind the steering wheel on the steering column. Figures 3.21 and 3.22 depict a clockspring that caught fire on a 2004 Ford SUV.

The greatest flammability factor of both electric seats and seat heaters is that there is usually a combustible or flammable secondary fuel available. Consumers will stuff all manner of combustibles under and next to seats. Prior to the advent of the high-density polyurethane seat foam (>PUR<, thermoset non-saturated), standard seat foam would support flaming combustion reasonably well, particularly if there were some maps or newspaper stuffed in the crack of the seat. Modern seats constructed from >PUR< will surround any flaming seat foam with NOx (oxide of nitrogen) gas as it burns. As soon as the secondary fuel is exhausted, the NOx gas snuffs the seat out because the inert nature of the gas has choked out any available oxygen at the area of ignition.

One area the investigating engineer should examine is the possible presence of snack chips on or near the seat that burned. The snack chips will render oil out of the product as the fire attacks the bag or box of snack chips. The oil will act as an accelerant. In simpler terms, snack chips will take a material that normally will combust rather poorly and turn it into an inferno that produces completely uncharacteristic burn patterns and transfer temperatures for the >PUR< material.

The critical analysis path for the investigating engineer here is to determine the root primary failed part. Determine the type of seat foam being used. Personal research and visits to wrecking yards are required to familiarize the investigator with the different materials commonly used in the different years of production.

The investigating engineer should be able to determine which modern vehicles will use >PUR-unsaturated thermoset< as the seat foam material, or use another composite embedded in the foam. In many cases, OEM seat foam is available as a vehicle part number which can be ordered from the parts department of the respective vehicle franchise. Otherwise, an exemplar seat can be procured from a wrecking yard for burn testing. Data can be recorded for use in a study and documentation of testing for any legal proceedings.

If the burn pattern indicates a high consumption of the >PUR-unsaturated< seat foam material, then it must be determined if a secondary fuel was available. This analysis should determine how much and what type of material was present. Paper and rags are the most common. However, experience has shown consumers carry all manner of materials in their vehicles. When the seat foam burns, the secondary fuel acts much like a wick does to a kerosene lamp. It will prolong the flaming combustion stage. The >PUR< material is highly noncombustible. It does not ignite or transfer heat well at all. If the material is badly destroyed, then the level of destruction must be explained or the condition should be regarded as suspicious. This material is discussed in greater detail in Section 4.5.

L. High current flow computer modules

These types of modules will typically be used for high current draw systems. These units are capable of powering and making real-time decisions for air-ride, hydraulic-ride, ABS, active stabilization systems, and some older memory seat modules.

Universally, if the cover is de-layered from a failed unit there will be large metal conductors, silicon-controlled rectifiers, power diodes, power transistors, and larger internal relays. The circuitry will appear larger in component size than normal integrated circuits found in other types of memory modules.

For example, a hydraulic ride control unit for level platform performance on cornering will have both large engagement relays and memory capacity to meet the design specifications of performance response (generally 90–130 milliseconds). If this unit were opened and compared to an engine control module, the difference in component size would be readily apparent.

Most non-current carrying computer modules equipped on modern vehicles will operate on 5 volts with a current draw in the milliamps range. These units do not draw sufficient current to start a fire. None of the input sensors are capable of starting a fire. If a fault develops, the unit either stops working or begins operating on a base program instruction (PROM).

The critical analysis path for the investigating engineer here is to determine if the module failed from internal or external influences. For example, a hypothetical failed circuit contains an electric motor. The analysis should include an examination of the circuit fuse, circuit relay (if so equipped), control module, circuit wiring loom, and electric motor to determine the greatest source of the electrical heat. A locked armature condition is found in the electric motor but the fire started in the relay panel. The primary failed part is the electric motor. The locked armature caused the circuit to heat up. The relay panel is the point of ignition, but not the cause of the fire.

The investigating engineer should be able to identify what the general characteristics are for the computer module being inspected just by looking at the type of circuitry components present. A good approach to gaining this experience is to visit wrecking yards to examine the different systems used by various manufacturers. "Known to be bad" modules can usually be purchased quite cheaply for destructive examination of the internal circuit boards.

In conclusion, the electrical fire originating from operational mode failure or from parked mode failure (primary key-off circuits) will typically result in a low order fire. However, this is not always true. If the fire has caused major damage, then the primary fuel and secondary fuel must be identified in addition to the identification of the primary failed part. If the fire involves more than one compartment, then the method of fire communication must be identified. If a secondary fuel was involved, then the BTU load potential from this source must be approximated. Notably, the only type of accidental fire which can occur inside the passenger compartment is an electrical fire. Fuel lines and flammable liquids are not normally present unless placed there by the owner or driver.

As discussed, most electrical fires merely flare up then snuff out. This is due to several factors. However, there is the possibility of the electrical fire causing a high order fire. For example, presume the Power Distribution Module (fuse and relay box) is located next to the brake fluid reservoir. It fails internally catching itself and nearby wiring insulation on fire. The flaming combustion would attack the nearby brake fluid reservoir. The brake fluid would heat up, then ignite into a large flaming plume that would quickly spread across the engine compartment. This scenario would likely result in heavy destruction inside the engine compartment with fire penetration and burn patterns moving rearward. Without the secondary fuel being present close by the electrical failure, then the most common result is the fire merely flares up then snuffs out for lack of fuel.

Since electrical fire is the most common type of fire, then the key to the correct analysis and determination of the primary failed part is for the investigating engineer to be familiar with the composites present and the flammability factors present at the point of origin. Basically, the questions will be, where was the point of origin and how was the spread of fire conducted? If the area of primary ignition can be successfully identified, then components with inherent fire propensity designs should be examined as the primary failed part. Even when the area of ignition is identified, there remains to be decided whether the component which was destroyed by electrical heat was the cause or a victim of the fire.

3.4 Add-On and Optional Equipment

In analyzing a fire claim, one of the areas which must be explored by the investigating engineer is whether or not the consumer has added any additional options or circuits to the existing OEM product.

The range of electrical optional equipment available on the aftermarket is substantial. Some common add-ons are stereos, alarm systems, premium sound systems, DVD and video players, fog and driving lamps, neon lights, electric rear area heaters, electric coolers, battery chargers, power inverters, hydraulic suspension, and electric camping equipment.

Figure 3.23

Figure 3.24

Many times the add-on equipment will be the cause of electrical heat in a circuit. For example, large amplifiers required for customized sound systems require so much amperage to run that a second battery and modified alternators with increased amperage output are commonly installed. These types of amplifiers are capable of consuming so much electricity that an ordinary car battery can be completely discharged in as little as 20 minutes.

Figures 3.23 and 3.24 depict a trunk fire in a 1996 Chevrolet Impala. The fire was caused by an improper installation of remote batteries for the stereo power amplifier system.

If the fire on the failed product is determined to be electrical in nature, then an evaluation must be made as to whether or not the primary failed part was due to aftermarket optional equipment, causing the circuit to fail.

Some examples of common failures are:

- Alternator failed because the custom stereo system ran the battery dead too many times. This concern is usually accompanied by warranty replacement of battery on multiple occasions.
- Multiple alternator failures due to lamps or a stereo power amplifier added to the circuit. Possible areas to investigate include trailer lamps and corroded trailer lamp connector sockets.

- Door fire because the aftermarket alarm system relay failed and held the electric door solenoid in the "on" position, causing circuit to overheat.
- Inverters or battery chargers plugged into the cigar lighter.
- Add-on "projector lamp" type headlamps.
  - Corroded trailer lamp socket. Also, poor trailer cord connector.
  - Too many lamps mounted on trailer.

The critical analysis path for the investigating engineer here is to examine the circuit for signs that aftermarket products have been installed or used by the driver. Aftermarket installations may be constructed using crimp connectors and line tap connectors. The fusible links or dedicated fuses for the added equipment circuit should be examined carefully. Many times the installation was not performed by a professional shop. Thus, the wiring may have formed a high resistance connection or has chafed its insulation causing an intermittent short. Any add-on relays should be disassembled and their casings carefully inspected to determine if the relay melted from the inside-outward or was burned by the fire from outside-inward. The investigations should include questions to the owner or driver regarding equipment that may have been plugged into the cigar lighter but now is not with the vehicle.

As previously discussed, most electrical circuits in an automobile do not have much redundancy designed into the circuit. The minimal AWG and connector type is selected to keep the weight of the vehicle down and to minimize costs. If the owner or driver adds an option to an existing circuit, it may cause the circuit to heat. Generally, there is only a 20–30 percent maximum redundancy factor in any circuit. That is to say, the circuit can only handle a load factor of up to 30 percent over the rated current capacity of the wire used without heating up and melting the insulation. However, many modern circuit designs have moved to a much lower redundancy factor. Typically, weight and cost are the driving factors in these decisions by an automobile manufacturer.

If the failure involved the cigar lighter circuit, it may be because it was used as a heat source. There is one unusual practice that has been associated with drug users. This practice involves holding the cigar lighter in past the point of self-release several times. The hot element is then used to burn the stub of a marijuana cigarette or to heat drugs for smoking or injection. This action will cause the cigar lighter circuit to overheat at the relay panel and at the connector behind the cigar lighter itself. Many times, there is a "V" burn pattern moving away from the back of the cigar lighter socket at the dashboard.

The investigating engineer should inspect the heating element for any signs that something other than an ordinary cigarette has come in contact with the element. Signs of overheating at the element may also include: de-tempering of the metal surrounding the heat element, melted portions of the heating element, or a slightly melted plastic knob. Melted insulation from the lighter socket to the source is another sign of cigar lighter abuse by the operator of the vehicle. The investigation should include an assessment of the cigar lighter element assembly to eliminate accidental lighter malfunction as the cause. The cigar lighter removable element should be verified as OEM, not an aftermarket replacement.

3.5 Gas Tank Systems

The gas tank on early vehicles was constructed from steel for virtually all makes and models. The basic tank was two stamped steel halves that were seam welded together. The fuel outlet could be located either at the top or the bottom of the tank.

If the vehicle is equipped with a carburetor and a mechanical fuel pump, a large pool of gasoline could potentially begin forming under the engine if the flexible gas hose that routed from the frame to the fuel pump nipple ruptured.

Another fire issue presents when a static electricity spark occurs during refueling. Many times the static charge develops when the consumer slides back and forth across the upholstery of the driver seat. If a static charge does develop as the consumer exits the vehicle while refueling, the static spark may ignite the gasoline vapors.

Polypropylene fuel tank styles began appearing in the late 1970s. Newer designs incorporate highly crosslinked polypropylene (>HCPP<) as the preferred material. Proprietary additive formulas for the plastic tank designs are common.

Static electricity is generated when gasoline flows over a plastic surface. Thus, most modern plastic gas tank designs will incorporate a ground wire as part of the design. Static electricity is not an issue with diesel fuel tanks because they generally are not grounded. However, an issue arises if the consumer inadvertently introduces gasoline into the diesel fuel tank. Many modern gas stations will now dispense diesel fuel from a separate fueling nozzle mounted alongside the gasoline dispensing nozzle. It is an easy mistake for a consumer to make by accidentally fueling a diesel vehicle with gasoline.

If a static electricity spark fire occurs inside a diesel fuel tank, the consumer may report a muffled noise that vaguely resembles an explosion, or may report flames spewing from the fuel filler neck.

Fuel tanks on early vehicles were commonly located in back of the rear axle. Some European designs located the gas tank in the front. Both of these designs allowed for collision emollition of the passengers due to a ruptured fuel tank.

In the event of gasoline being mixed in with the diesel, send a sample of the suspected fuel to an oil analysis lab for spectrochemical analysis. This will confirm elements of gasoline are present in the diesel fuel.

Modern fuel tanks will commonly be located in front of the rear axle either in a horizontal or vertical orientation. Newer gas tank filler necks will commonly incorporate a gas cap that is designed to separate into two halves if a collision event occurred to the fuel neck area. The inner portion that screws into the filler neck separates from the outside half. This helps prevent fuel leakage during a collision event.

The latest fuel filler neck design is not equipped with a gas tank cap. There is merely a spring-loaded flap over the inside of the filler. On these designs, there is a large metal ball contained within a cage inside the filler neck. If the vehicle should become involved in a rollover collision, the metal ball will roll toward the opening in the fuel filler neck, preventing the fuel from leaking.

Many modern rear-wheel drive vehicles will be configured with a "saddle" style fuel tank. This design is actually two tanks that sit on either side of the driveshaft. The design looks similar to saddle bags on a horse. The fuel filler neck will fill one side up, and the crossover portion allows the fuel to spill over into the other side. When the engine is running, there are two fuel pumps operating. One will move the fuel from one tank to the other, while the other fuel pump moves the fuel up to the engine.

Regardless of fuel tank design, if the fuel system ruptured as part of the fire event, the investigator should be knowledgeable about the tank designs and how they operate.

3.6 Evaporative Emissions Systems

"Evaporative Emissions" (EVAP) appears in all modern fuel tank systems. The early EVAP systems were vacuum operated. Essentially, the fumes from the top of the gas tank were sucked into the intake manifold using manifold vacuum.

As most advanced EVAP systems began appearing after 1996, the systems became electronic. A sensor was mounted in the tank to assist with the EVAP cycle. Generally, the systems will operate below 3/4 of a tank and above 1/4 tank of fuel. The computer determines if the fuel tank is within the desired range of fuel. The tank is either pressurized via a small electric motor, or a vacuum is placed on the tank air space.

If the pressure (or vacuum) sensor in the tank relays to the Powertrain Control Module (PCM) that the tank kept pressure (or vacuum) longer than the minimum time programmed, then the PCM will send a signal to the "purge" solenoid. The purge solenoid will open, allowing the fumes from the gas tank to be drawn through an activated charcoal filter and into the engine. After cycling, the system merely goes back to sleep until another drive cycle is initiated.

There are other EVAP system designs that will "wake up" the vehicle somewhere between 2-7 hours after shut down. The tank is pressurized. A specified timeout period must pass. If the engine computer determines that the tank has not returned to atmospheric pressure after the timeout period has passed, then the system will pull the vapors from the top of the tank and isolate them in an activated charcoal filter. The next time the engine is started, the stored vapors are pulled into the engine via manifold vacuum from the intake manifold.

Most of the time, the advanced EVAP system components are located in the rear by the filler neck. Earlier systems located the components in the engine compartment.

Regardless of where the charcoal canister is located, if the investigation determines that the unit was full of raw gasoline, the investigating engineer can presume that the system was malfunctioning. The EVAP system could very well be a causal or contributing factor in the fire.

If the fire appears to have originated from the EVAP system, the tip for the investigating engineer is to procure the workshop manual information on how the EVAP system operates for the model being investigated.

3.7 Electrical Fire Evidence

When an add-on or OEM wire has heated sufficiently or has shorted to ground on an unfused positive wire such that the insulation has caught fire, then a greenish coating known as copper sulfide, sulfate, or copper chloride, may form over the wire which had its core temperature raised to high or near melting temperature. This discolored formation is most closely associated with the affected wire having insulation comprised from polyvinyl chloride (PVC). The formation is not commonly associated with wire coated with polyethylene plastics (PE). The formation of the greenish coating is due to the chloride converting to an acid in the presence of heat and water. Hydrochloric acid is formed in this example.

Lab testing may also indicate the presence of copper sulfate. This is due to the battery outgassing sulfuric acid molecules during charging, the battery exploding, or the casing melting as a factor in the fire. In this example, the acid is spewed or leaked into the wiring around the battery. The sulfuric acid from the battery electrolyte reacts with the copper wiring and moisture from a fire hose or evening dew. A blue/green coating will form. There is some dispute in the application of this theory.

In order to resolve some of the disputes on this subject, this author has conducted testing on inducement of direct shorts and overheated circuits (wire overload testing by this author, 2007 and 2012). The test parameters involved the use of standard automotive wires taken from various automotive wiring looms. Some of the test wires had polyvinyl chloride (PVC) insulation while others were insulated with polyethylene (PE). Different AWG wire sizes were subjected to destructive current capacities (ampacity) and the copper compounds being formed was measured.

The test conditions included load testing using an automotive battery alone to simulate a parked vehicle and with a charger on the battery to simulate the presence of an alternator. The wire sizes selected for testing were AWG #10, #12, #14, #16 and #18. Wires were tested singularly and contained within pieces of automotive wiring looms cut from scrap vehicles. All test pieces were placed in a loaded dead-short test jig such that the weakest point would be the test wire. The current flow in the circuit was raised using a conventional carbon-pile load tester until the melting point in the wire was reached.

After either the wire burned through, the insulation was consumed, or the unassisted battery ran dead, the test wires were left outside so that the dew of the night would collect on the wire. All of the test samples with PVC insulation or accumulated battery acid on the insulation formed copper sulfide, copper chloride, or copper sulfate. The samples with PE insulation did not form any discoloration or coating. Some of the copper wiring formed red and black oxides of copper.

These testing results run counter to the conclusions reached in other published fire studies where discoloration or copper sulfide formations on wires are stated to be meaningless. The 2011 Edition of NFPA 921 states that PVC insulation is associated with the formation of greenish copper sulfides or copper chlorides due to acid formation during the fire event.

However, it should be noted that the studies researched were all based on AC electricity not DC electricity as found in automotive circuits. Additionally, automobiles are wired with stranded-type wire. Moreover, underhood wiring on vehicles is subject to the accumulation of road grime, heat, battery acid vapor outgassing, and vibration. House wiring is not a true comparison to automotive wiring.

Road grime is an accumulation of oils, dirt, metal dust, tire dust, brake shoe/pad dust, oxides of all manner, water, and so on. Accumulated road grime can conduct electricity. It is a common auto shop experiment for the instructor to place the positive lead of a volt meter on the battery positive and touch the negative lead into the road grime accumulation on the top of a vehicle battery. The meter will register a current path on all but the cleanest of battery tops. Figures 3.25 and 3.26 depict a meter indicating a path to ground across the plastic top of a battery.

The instructor will touch differing parts of the nearby plastics to show current path potential. The vehicle being tested will generally show slight paths to ground. The possibility of road grime creating an improper path to ground is one reason a technician should perform the voltage drop test described in section 3.3.B, *Alternator fires*.

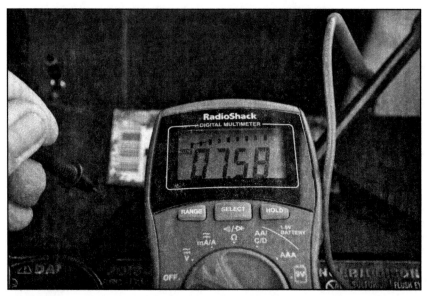

Figure 3.25 *Volt meter reading through road grime on top of battery.*

Figure 3.26 *Volt meter testing at battery terminals.*

The wire used in the other fire research testing by NFPA and other engineers was solid-type house wiring. The test wiring was subjected to the temperatures achieved with wood and other combustibles present in the test houses burned. This subjects the wiring to a completely different heat range than the combustibles and polymeric composites which comprise the interior of an automobile. Any such research data discovered by the investigating engineer should be carefully examined to determine that the testing environment is representative of that found in a burning automobile.

"Arc beading" is a condition associated with high electrical heat. This is characterized by a melted drip of copper at the site where the shorting wire parted. Rarely will a wire be melted in an arc beading fashion when exposed to the normal transfer temperatures encountered in automotive fire. Even the accelerated temperatures encountered with the ignition of a flammable liquid will not cause an arc bead by convection or radiant heat. This condition is generally associated with a direct electrical short-to-ground. However, a sustained high heat release rate such as some wiring being impinged by a burning tire or combustible fluid may create the temperatures required to melt the copper strands. Figures 3.27 and 3.28 are examples of stranded copper wiring that was attacked by a burning tire during a vehicle fire. In this example, both of the two battery positive cables were routed

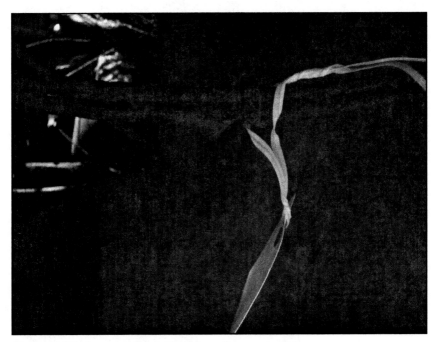

Figure 3.27 Copper wire melted by a fire on an RV.

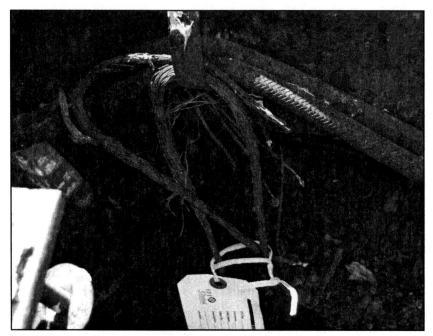

Figure 3.28 Copper wire melted by electrical heat.

along the frame in the wheel house next to the left front tire on an RV fire. The destruction site and type were different for the two cables even though they were physically located about 12 inches from each other.

There are two main theories in current use for determining if the arc bead discovered is a causal factor or a victim of the fire. The first theory holds that the investigating engineer can take the arc bead sample to the lab for testing. The most common types of testing employed are light microscopy, scanning electron microscope, dispersive X-ray, or gas chromatograph/mass spectrometer (GC/MS).

The arc bead is examined first on the surface layers for the presence of combustion material embedded in the surface molecules. Next, the surface molecules are removed and the sample is retested. If there are more combustion materials present in the melted alloy, this indicates that the wire was a victim of another heat source.

The second theory holds that the wire is surrounded by a polyvinyl or polyethylene coating which contains many of the same carbon and hydrocarbon chains as does a flammable liquid or is found in elements of flaming combustion of automotive composites. Even if the insulation is consumed by heat before the arc bead forms, it will mix with the melting alloy from the beginning of the softening of the copper due to heat impingement.

Figure 3.29 John Deere tractor battery fire.

Figure 3.30 John Deere tractor battery fire.

Another issue that is subject to argument is that stranded copper wire becomes brittle when exposed to high-order heat from a fire or electrical heat. As noted, the copper strands will commonly form a ruddish-red or black oxide on the copper. This occurs when high electrical heat is present in the failed wire. Commonly, the strand bundles on larger cables such as battery cables will begin to untwist. The bundling of the strands begins to fall apart. If handled, the copper strands are brittle and might break easily.

Figures 3.29 and 3.30 depict the battery box on a John Deere tractor that suffered an electrical fire. The fire occurred in the middle of a farm field. It merely burned itself out. Thus, there was no interference from fire department personnel. These battery cables appear just as they did when the failure occurred. No one has touched the batteries or cables. Note the untwisting of the cable bundles particularly in the battery positive cable.

The difficulty arises in defining with certainty whether electricity was the cause of the heat, or the wire was impinged with heat. The investigating engineer or fire investigator will not know the extent to which any evidence was damaged by fire department personnel extinguishing the fire.

As noted above and in NFPA 921,[27] an arc bead on the end of a conductor does not indicate the cause of the fire in and of itself. Moreover, if something is pulling on the deteriorating copper stranded cable, then the appearance of the wire ends will be sharp. For example, an engine fire is attacking the battery. The battery is dislodged from its pedestal. The weight of the battery is now pulling on the battery cables. If sufficient heat is generated, whether it is convective or electrical, then the ends of the wire strands affected will show points when examined with a microscope.

The critical analysis path for the investigating engineer is to proceed with caution and to not lend credence to any one factor over another. The conclusion should be drawn based on all evidence gathered.

3.8 Normal Burn Temperatures and Burn Patterns

Almost every substance on earth contains carbon in some form. If subjected to a high enough level of heat, almost everything will burn. Items thought to be not flammable such as steel and concrete become flammable if exposed to a 6,000–7,000°F fire. Throwing pieces of concrete and pouring water into such a fire would be much like throwing more logs and gasoline on a campfire. The question to answer is what created such a hot fire in the first place.

As previously discussed, the earlier vehicles and the composites from which they were constructed were considerably more combustible and would sustain flaming combustion fairly easily. Later-models vehicles, particularly luxury vehicles, are constructed from materials which are nearly impossible to ignite during an operational mode failure. Even if some ignition occurred, the burning composite in the area of ignition would surround itself with NOx as the flames were occurring and the combustion would snuff out.

Thus, the most important first conclusion that the investigating engineer must determine is the BTU potential fire load for the area where the fire started. Subsequently, the fire communication path must be defined. If the vehicle being investigated is constructed from early materials or is a recreational vehicle, then there exists the possibility of a flashover fire from smoldering materials. The minimum size fire that can cause a flashover in a given area is a function of the ventilation provided through an opening. This function is known as the "ventilation factor" and is calculated as the area of the opening times the square root of the height of the opening.

An approximation of the heat release rate for flashover can be found from the following relationship:[27]

$$HRR_{fo}(kW) = (750A_o)(h_o)0.5$$

where

HRR_{fo} = heat release rate for flashover
A_o = area of opening (square meters)
h_o = height of opening (meters)

The same formula expressed in English units is

$$HRR_{fo}(BTU/s) = 18.4A_o(h_o)0.5 + 0.69A_w$$

where

HRR_{fo} = heat release rate for flashover
A_o = area of opening (square feet)
h_o = height of opening (feet)
A_w = area of walls, ceiling, and floor (square meters)

Flashover is only a factor in a vehicle fire where materials of a fairly flammable or combustible nature are present and exposed to a heat source sufficient to cause smoldering combustion. Sometimes the smoking and vaporous cloud which precludes flashover is referred to as "flammable carbon monoxide." Regardless, flashover fire is a result of the ignition of suspended VOCs in the heat plume which are ignited suddenly due to the presence of piloted ignition or superheated gasses. Introduction of oxygen may be the cause of the flashover.

Approximate smoldering time of 1.5–2 hours is generally required for flaming combustion to erupt. Not all vehicle interior materials are required to be FMVSS 302 compliant. Automotive seats are designed to resist cigarettes and matches. However, RV seating or the sleeper portion of a Class 8 heavy truck may be constructed from household-type composites. The time from the dropping of the cigarette or proximity of combustible material to the heat source to the actual eruption of flames has been studied and documented to be approximately 1.5–2 hours for most household materials.[9]

For example, a carelessly discarded cigarette lands on the kitchen table seat pad of an RV. It will immediately begin melting the material until the remaining tobacco is exhausted or snuffs out. At some point, flaming combustion occurs after a period of smoldering. If a carelessly discarded cigarette lands on an automotive seat, all that happens is that the seat foam melts where the cigarette landed. Flaming combustion is rare without a secondary fuel (such as a map) present.

In the example involving a cigarette, most states have enacted laws regarding elimination of potassium nitrate from the cigarette formula. This creates a cigarette that tends to snuff out. However, smoldering combustion may have begun before the cigarette went out.

As a general rule, operational mode fire is very small. Only a section of the vehicle is involved. Fire investigations must rule out all accidental sources of fire before the fire investigation begins to focus on incendiary fires.

The operational mode failure can occur during operation or when parked. A system merely needs to be on to satisfy the definition of operational mode failure. The position of the ignition key is not relevant.

The most conducive fire to analyze is one in which the flames were extinguished early. A vehicle can reach a point of destruction in which the consumption of composites has obliterated all the evidence. There may not be enough remaining evidence to make a determination with any confidence.

There is an adage in fire investigation which applies more to structure fire than to automotive fire. It states that the source of the fire is the area with the least destruction. This presumes that there are ordinary combustibles present at the start of the burn. As the fire grows, the destruction level increases in proportion to the amount of combustibles. Many times a "V" pattern will show up as the path of destruction going up a wall.

The investigation of automotive fires is somewhat opposite to the adage of structure fires. This is particularly true with newer and luxury vehicles. Flame retardant composites will tend to contain the fire to the source area. Due to compartment construction and flame retardant composites, there will rarely be an observable "V" pattern. Thus, many times the area of origin is the area with the most destruction. This practice is known as fire or burn pattern identification. Burn pattern identification and heat transfer ability of the fire are essential to identifying the primary failed part.

Fire has the propensity to burn upward. It must have oxygen, fuel to consume, and a space in which to propagate. If none of these conditions is met, the flames merely snuff out. Before flaming combustion can occur in an automobile, a source of primary ignition and primary fuel must occur. Given the propensity of newer polymerics and composites to not propagate flames, any significant fire requires that a secondary fuel source be readily available.

Inspect the height of the point of ignition and material consumption. Most sources of automotive fire are under the hood or inside the dashboard. Both sources will create a point of ignition high in the profile view of the vehicle. If the fire is in the engine compartment, then the flame burn pattern will tend to be on the upper portion of the motor. If the fire has burned down low on the frame or underneath the vehicle, then the cause for this type of burn pattern must be found. Fire burn patterns will always move upwards unless the flames are forced downward or the fire occurred low on the vehicle.

If the fire erupted in the engine compartment and there is some ingress into the passenger compartment, then the duct through the firewall must have been large enough to have allowed fire penetration. If the only holes in the firewall are small passages for the HVAC heater core and evaporator lines, then fire propagation under the dash is not likely unless the parameters for a positive pressure fire have forced the fire through the holes with sufficient heat transfer to destroy the coolant hose or aluminum A/C line first. Additionally, there must be sufficient conductive heat transfer to cause the components on the other side of the firewall to begin supporting flaming combustion.

Determining fire burn pattern requires experience in automobile fire, the construction of the materials involved, and the ability to define the approximate quantity of BTU potential load in the affected area of the automobile. One suggestion for garnering experience in automobile fire patterns is for the investigating engineer to visit wrecking yards and insurance auto salvage disposal auctions and inspect the vehicles deemed a total loss by fire.

The investigating engineer should not fall into the trap of using any one single piece of evidence extracted from the fire debris. The analysis should be supported by as many indicators as possible, a sound knowledge of the BTU load potential of the materials affected, and the operating specifications of the affected systems.

To define the heat potential of a given fire, the best method is to first identify the heat transfer requirements of the different materials consumed. For example, if the fire evidence includes consumed composites but no damage to surrounding aluminum components then it can be deduced that the transfer temperature of the fire was in the 400–700°F range.

Table 3.3
Melting Point of Common Automotive Materials[2,27]

Material	Melting Point °F	Ignition Point °F
Aluminum (alloys)	1,050–1,200	1,220
Aluminum (pure billet)	1,220	1,832
Aluminum pot metal	875–1,000	1,220
ABS	190–257	871
Brass (yellow)	1,710	—
Cast iron	2,460–2,550	—
Chromium	3,350	—
Copper	1,981	—
Fiberglass (polyester resin)	802–932	1,040
Glass (general types)	1,100–260	—
Auto safety glass	1,200–1,400	—
Steel (carbon)	2,100–2,760	—
Steel (stainless)	2,000–2,600	—
Solder	275–350	—
Tin	449	—
Zinc	707	—

Note: The temperatures recorded are only an average for the element tested. These figures are not intended to be anything but a general guide for the transfer temperature required to melt or consume the element. Reprinted with permission from NFPA 921-2001, Guide for Fire and Explosion Investigation, Copyright © 2001, NFPA, Quincy, MA. This reprinted material is not the complete and official position of the NFPA on the referenced subject, which is represented by the standard in its entirety.

Table 3.3 shows the different melting points of common materials found in an automobile or truck.

The two materials which should be given careful attention are aluminum components, aluminum pot metal castings such as found on intake manifolds or the steering column housing, and the window glass. If these materials are substantially consumed, then this is an indication that an extremely hot fire with good transfer capabilities was present.

Another factor to note is the alloy and mass of the aluminum. "Pot" metal aluminum is simply a common term for aluminum that has been mixed with unknown quantities of other metals such as tin and zinc. This type of aluminum alloy will begin melting at a lower temperature than stronger alloys of aluminum such as ASTM 6160 or 6173. The mass of the aluminum component should also be considered. For example, most of the time the alternator will survive an engine compartment fire pretty much intact unless failure from within the alternator was the cause. This is due to the mass of the alternator. The fire must be able to communicate sufficient sustained heat to the mass to make it melt.

It should also be noted that the materials equipped on entry-level vehicles which are barely FMVSS 302 compliant may sustain burning combustion with sufficient transfer temperatures to substantially melt the steering column where later-model vehicles will not.

Another sign of an uncharacteristically hot fire is if there are pools of melted windshield glass dripped down in low areas. As of the date of this printing, side windows and rear windows are only made from tempered glass not safety glass. These windows show a propensity for shattering when subjected to significant heat that occurs over a longer timeframe. Melted pools of glass found clinging to the door, down inside the door, or pooled next to the door is an indicator of an abnormal heat release rate was present (i.e., an accelerant).

The normal transfer temperature of burning polymeric plastics that have a nonflammable rating will not generate a sufficient enough heat release rate to cause much damage to surrounding window glass. Simply put, if the windows are up on a car fire originating in the passenger compartment, the sheer amount of NOx and smoke generated will choke out the flaming combustion in most cases. An open window or another source of air is required for the flames to propagate.

Typically, automotive fire will affect only one portion of the vehicle. The entire vehicle will not be consumed. If the fire originates at or spread to the fuel tank, the pattern should be underneath the vehicle in the general drain direction of the road on which the vehicle caught fire. A visit to the fire site will be required to determine the direction of drainage of the road.

When a metal gas tank ruptures from heat expansion and a large order fire ensues, this will cause a boiling liquid evaporating vapor explosion (BLEVE). The boiling liquid gasoline will typically build pressure, spew out the filler neck and, possibly, out of the fuel pump tubes. If a polypropylene (plastic) fuel tank is equipped, then a BLEVE will not occur. The plastic will melt through long before the gasoline has a chance to reach boiling temperatures or for burst pressure to build. The tank will merely dump the flaming gasoline out onto the road.

The critical analysis path for the investigating engineer is to determine the center of the greatest source of heat, the heat release rate, and the fire communication pathway. The primary failed part is almost always located within the fire epicenter area. This is determined by tracing the area of least damage back to the area of greatest damage. If the fire began as a large order fire, then there should be some type of flammable liquid in the epicenter of the burn area. The fire will radiate outward in a manner consistent with the available fuel or heat release rate of the surrounding composites. If the fire was electrical in nature, the damage should be quite limited unless there was a flammable liquid or other combustible close by which was ignited by the melting circuitry.

3.9 Arson Indicators

Arson is a crime. It can be perpetrated for a number of reasons. Financial gain, to get rid of a lemon automobile, jealousy, retaliation, or a fascination with fire are just a few reasons.

The investigating engineer's principal job is to determine if there exists a primary failed part which could have caused an operational mode fire. If the evidence gathered does not indicate a failed part or accidental cause for the fire, then the possibility of an incendiary fire must be explored. However, the utmost caution must be exercised in making this determination as criminal charges or an adverse report may be issued by the local authorities or the insurance carrier for the subject vehicle.

The most common mistake a perpetrator makes in arson is that a copious quantity of a flammable liquid is splashed around the interior or the engine compartment and then ignited. The result will be a burn pattern which will be obviously greater than the available fuel load.

It should be noted that the only type of fire which can occur inside the passenger area is an electrical one. Fuel lines do not run through the passenger compartment. They will be routed underneath the vehicle. If a fuel-based fire is suspected, then an entry point for the fuel to enter the passenger compartment must be found or incendiary fire must be concluded.

A ruptured gasoline tank under the vehicle may very well deposit elements of gasoline (like napthalene) into the cabin area. The heated air containing gasoline molecules will entrain through the vehicle. It is possible that some of the gasoline vapor molecules are drawn through broken windows to be deposited on the interior. If a sample is taken from interior materials to be sent to a lab for GC/MS testing, this may produce a false positive. See Figure 3.31 for a read-out from a GC/MS test containing gasoline.

There may be a reasonable explanation for the presence of gasoline in the passenger compartment. For example, the driver of the subject vehicle may be carrying gasoline in plastic milk jugs on the seat of the vehicle. While this may not be the smartest practice, it is not illegal. If an electrical fire should happen to occur and ignite the fuel jug, then an uncharacteristic fire burn pattern will result. However, the cause is not arson.

The most important point for the investigating engineer to realize is that all sources of accidental fire cause must be eliminated before moving the fire analysis into the incendiary fire rationale. The determination of arson must be made with absolute certainty.

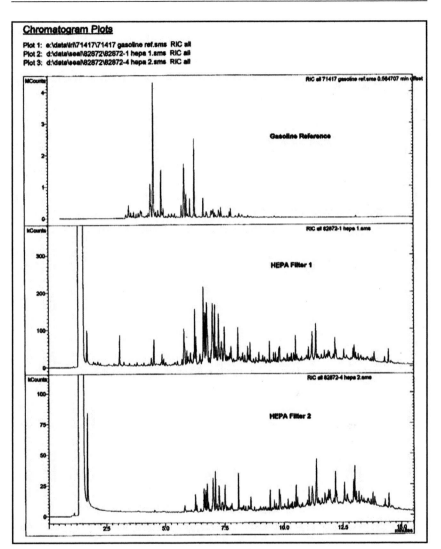

Figure 3.31 *A GC/MS test containing gasoline.*

There is a tool in common use for field investigation called a "combustible gas detector." Sometimes this tool is commonly called a "sniffer." This device detects the presence of flammable gasses and hydrocarbons. The device will have a small internal vacuum to suck air across an infrared field or an "eddy" current. The amount of infrared or the amount of current absorbed and the speed with which it crosses the sample are electronically measured. If flammable gas or vapor is detected, then an alarm is sounded. Precaution should be used with these devices as they are prone to a false triggering. These units operate best when the batteries in the unit are fresh and the proper calibration procedure per manufacturer's instructions is followed before use.

Simply pressing the air intake screen up against a foam or fabric test sample will usually result in a false reading. The units must be able to flow air across the element surface. If airflow is choked off then most units will emit a false trigger. These units are designed to test air samples of vapors contained in ordinary air. Most units require that the air sample be no closer than 0.5 inch to any flat surface which can choke off the air flow. If the unit is being used on a round surface such as a pipe, the sample screen can be touched to the sample area because the round surface of the pipe will not choke off the airflow.

When the combustible gas detector is first used, the operator should familiarize himself with the unit's sensitivity to different commonly procured flammable liquids. These units respond differently when the element is exposed to gasoline, paint thinner, lighter fluid, acetone, lacquer thinner and other common flammable liquids. Most units will have a multistage trigger level. The higher the aromatic value of the flammable gas, the quicker the highest trigger level is reached. A fresh air sample is required between each test. This will clear the element area of any contaminating molecules of the other samples before testing the next flammable liquid. These units will also respond to the presence of propane, butane, and methane (natural gas).

It is possible that accelerant residue may remain trapped inside seat foam or carpet padding. A common field use of the combustible gas detector is to place a remaining sample of seat foam or carpet padding in a plastic garbage bag. The sample should be exposed to direct sunlight for approximately 30 minutes. The sample may give up some flammable hydrocarbon vapors from the inside of the foam or padding layers which will now be detectable to the combustible gas detector when the air inside the bag is sampled.

Anytime a sample piece of evidence is suspected to contain an accelerant, it should be tested at a fire evidence testing laboratory for the presence of a flammable hydrocarbon. Unused paint cans, sold at most paint and hardware stores, are commonly used to gather and ship fire evidence. The interior of the can is clean and the lid provides a hermetic seal. A shipping label and postage can be affixed to the exterior.

3.10 Signs of Arson

Arson is the act of placing a flammable liquid or other flammable material in or near a vehicle and deliberately setting a fire. There are several signs which are commonly associated with vehicle fire due to arson:

- Whitish coating on steel panels
- Burn patterns low on the rockers or frame
- Melted pools of windshield or other window glass down to the floor
- Extreme heat and consumption of polymeric composites
- Fire burning under the engine or floor pan inconsistent with fuel load
- Fire in different compartments without direct communication route
- Complete destruction of steering column housing
- Destruction of large aluminum castings

A. Whitish coating

The whitish coating found on the exterior burned panels is the zinc oxide coming to the surface from either the hot galvanizing, cold galvanizing, or electro-deposition coating process. These processes are used by manufacturers to weatherproof the metal and prevent "flash" corrosion during the construction of the automobile. Most manufacturers utilize a vertical dip tank containing zinc phosphate. The raw vehicle is completely immersed into the solution prior to paint and assembly. The vehicle is grounded while the solution is positively charged. This causes the zinc molecules to migrate to the vehicle and adhere to every surface immersed in the zinc phosphate bath.

Hot galvanizing and cold galvanizing coatings are adhered to bare metal under a hot dip process. Hot galvanizing and electro-deposition coatings are adhered to the base metal at temperatures of up to 750–850°F. For the zinc oxide to become separated from the base metal, the metal must be reheated to the approximate temperature at which the coating was applied. From this it can be deduced that the transfer temperature of the fire was fairly high.

Early plastics and upholstery materials could generate this type of heat over large surface areas, but not down low on the vertical panels. Normal transfer temperature of a modern polymeric composite generally will not generate sufficient heat to even burn the exterior paint to any significant degree. The heat release rate of the newer nonflammable nanocomposites under ordinary failure fire will barely even scorch the paint on the outside panels. Zinc oxide extraction over large areas of a vehicle's vertical panels where the composites are known to be nonflammable rated, is a sign of the presence of an accelerant.

B. Low burn patterns

Fire will always burn upward unless forced downward by some outside force. Low burn patterns found on areas such as the tread plate, door jamb, and lower rocker panel of a door known to be closed during the burn is a sign of the presence of an accelerant. The accelerant tends to run down between the door and the door jamb or tread plate as it is poured over the interior of the vehicle. When the accelerant is ignited, it will burn the paint off of the area in-between the closed door. The affected area may even get hot enough to extract the zinc oxide from the metal.

Paint has poor flammability. It must be burned by something else. When low burn patterns such as these are encountered, the evidence should be viewed with suspicion. Flaming combustion will not normally enter the tiny space between a closed door and the door jamb as there is insufficient space to support the combustion. However, the heat plume from a flaming accelerant will have little difficulty in creating this burn pattern. The rubber door seal is consumed either from direct contact of accelerant running down into that space or because the positive pressure environment surrounding the flaming accelerant pushes the heat plume against the seal. Once the seal has been consumed, the positive pressure will push the heat plume into the space between the closed door and the door jamb.

Other areas to inspect for low burn patterns are the lower tie bar of the core support, the front frame extensions, melted aluminum wheels suspension components, and under the floor of the vehicle. If there are signs of extreme heat in these areas that does not match the available fuel load, then an accelerant may have been present for the burn to reach the high temperatures evidenced.

C. Melted pools of glass

Windshield glass melts into pools around 1,100–1,400°F. Since the glass surrounds the passenger compartment, there should be very minimal glass damage in an accidental fire. Shattering of tempered glass can occur but not melted pools of glass. As discussed, the older vehicles were equipped with plastics that had greater flammability factors. Newer plastics are virtually nonflammable. If there are melted pools dripping from dash surfaces or at the floor, then this is an indicator that an extremely hot and aggressive fire was present. Even if the more flammable plastics that are barely FMVSS 302 compliant are present, these materials will not create the extreme heat necessary to form pools of melted glass. Pools of melted glass are usually signs of an accelerant.

It should be noted that the side window glass and rear window glass are only tempered glass. If the temperature inside the vehicle rises too quickly compared to the core or outside temperature of the glass, then this will likely result in shattering glass. If the impingement of heat on the glass is high over a slightly longer timeframe, then the potential to form pools of melted glass occurs.

Another sign of high, sudden high heat attacking the windshield is the center plastic (polyvinyl butylrate) will bubble between the two layers of glass. Some cracks may appear in the glass layers.

Given a long enough exposure to high heat, the windshield will commonly melt into pools found on the dashboard, dashboard frame, or other remaining structures after the fire is extinguished.

The investigating engineer should be sure to check inside the doors to determine if there are any signs of melted glass and whether or not the window regulators are in the up position. If all the windows and doors are closed at the moment of ignition on an interior fire, then this should choke off the oxygen necessary for a fire to gain a foothold.

D. Extreme consumption of polymerics

An accidental fire must progress in a spread pattern across the vehicle. There will be an area of greater consumption of the polymeric composites progressing to lesser consumption. If all or most of the interior plastics and dashboard are consumed, then this is a sign that an accelerant was present.

FMVSS 302 requires interior materials not to burn at a rate of greater than 102 mm per minute. This means that a fire will take 10–30 minutes or more to consume all of the foam material of an average seat. The fire must jump from seat to seat and continue with consumption of the material until the fire is extinguished.

Since automotive fires will produce extreme amounts of thick black smoke, they will tend to attract attention quickly. The approximate burn time can be deduced by the response time and extinguish time contained in the fire department report. Extreme or complete consumption of polymeric composites in apparently very short periods of time is a sign that an accelerant was present. Minimally, this type of evidence should be viewed with suspicion.

E. Fire burning under engine or floor pan

Caution should be exercised in the assessment of burning patterns under the engine or floor pan. First, the on-board flammable liquids such as power steering fluid, gasoline, transmission fluid, engine oil, and coolant should be checked to determine if any of these lines have ruptured. Many times the fire does not burn any of the on-board fluid reservoirs through. The presence of burning under the engine or floor pan when none of the on-board flammable liquids have contributed to the burn is a sign that an accelerant was present. Sometimes a perpetrator will stuff balls of newspaper or a plastic bag of accelerant under the vehicle prior to lighting it on fire. The paper will usually result in very minor burning with no rupture of the on-board flammable liquids. The plastic bag with accelerant may cause complete destruction particularly if placed under the fuel tank.

F. Fire in different compartments

Fire must burn in a direct pathway. Accidental fire will always progress from the area of greatest damage to the area of least damage unless somehow the fuel tank ignited and acted as an accountable accelerant. A burn pattern which is in two different places with no method of communication via convection, conduction, or radiant heat sources is a sign of the presence of an accelerant. In making this assessment, the investigating engineer should take into account any cargo the vehicle was carrying which might be more flammable than the materials the vehicle is constructed from.

G. Destruction of steering column

The steering column on most vehicles is a large aluminum casting. To destroy this piece means that a fire which was capable of transferring huge amounts of heat directly to a fairly dense casting occurred underneath or very near the sides of the steering column. Inside the aluminum housing is a steel shaft. Typically, this shaft is not damaged.

If the aluminum housing of the steering column has been completely consumed from the heat of the fire, this indicates that a fire with an ability to sustain 1,000°F for period of approximately three to five minutes occurred at just below dashboard level. Most manufacturers will utilize an alloy of aluminum to construct the steering column housing. As a general rule, AISI 6160 aluminum is not used in steering column housings. Therefore, the melting temperature of the material will be below the 1,100°–1,200°F required to melt stronger aluminum alloys.

Fire behavior is such that the flames will conduct heat upward and out any available aperture such as a broken or open window. Most of the heat will occur in the VOC's being released into the heat layer at or above the window level. This means that most of the heat will occur above the level of the steering column. If the column is completely consumed, this is a potential sign that an accelerant was located below the steering column during the burn.

H. Destruction of large aluminum castings

This part of the analysis deals with underhood components. Manufacturers will use aluminum castings on intake manifolds, alternator housings, throttle body components, A/C compressor housing and brackets, master cylinder, and suspension components.

If the fire's path of destruction includes the consumption of large aluminum castings, then the reason for this must be considered. This evidence indicates that a fire with a high transfer temperature occurred at that level on the engine. The engine compartment by design will cause the flames to diffuse outward-seeking oxygen and space in which to exist. The flames will be aimed down at the front grille, out at the wheel house area, and into the firewall.

Most of the time a flammable liquid will pool somewhere in or under the engine compartment near where its reservoir ruptures. This will produce a burn pattern wherever the fluid flows and continues to support burning combustion.

If the aluminum casting which is consumed is in this area or is in an area where the convecting heat could cause this type of destruction, then this is a normal pattern. If the aluminum castings which are consumed are nowhere near a flammable liquid, then this is a sign that there was an accelerant present.

To understand the characteristics of accelerant-based fire, the investigating engineer should have a solid understanding of the BTU load potential for under-hood flammable liquids and gasses. Table 3.4 compiles the flash points of common ignitable liquids and fuels for motor vehicles.

The critical analysis path for the investigating engineer is to understand that a finding of an incendiary fire will cause a report to be generated by the vehicle owner's insurance carrier to the National Insurance Crime Bureau. There may be a special criminal investigation by the Office of the District Attorney, state or local fire authority, or the Special Investigations Unit of the insurance carrier.

Utmost care must be taken when this type of report is issued. All aspects of accidental fire must be examined in detail and eliminated as the causal factor. There must be no finding of a primary failed part. The evidence gathered must be both compelling and exclusive of the possibility of any accidental cause.

Many states require the investigator to hold a local private investigator license in order to investigate the cause and origin of a fire. This can be conducted with the services of a private investigator teamed with the investigating engineer.

There is a valid argument that such laws will not stand up in court. Many states have a waiver clause written into their private investigator regulations that waive the license requirement for filed superior courts actions. Essentially, such codes state that a private investigator is somehow more qualified to assist in the analysis of a failed technical part than is the engineer who designed the product. Further, there is the argument that a section of the state business and professions code requiring a private investigator license runs counter to evidentiary codes whereby expert witnesses are called on to act in the capacity of assisting the trier of fact. Basically, the argument questions which code section is more relevant to assisting the court. Most courts will allow fire experts to testify without a private investigator license.

3.11 Alternative Technology
A. Bi-fuel vehicle
A bi-fuel vehicle runs on two different fuels, for example, gasoline and liquid natural gas. These vehicles are currently in production. However, they are not commonly found in the U.S. market. This fuel platform is preferred in European and third-world nations. The appropriate valves are set and the vehicle is operated on whichever fuel is available. These vehicles will commonly have two gas filler flaps: one for gasoline and one for natural gas.

B. Flex-fuel vehicle
A flex-fuel vehicle differs from a bi-fuel vehicle in that the engine and fuel management system are configured to operate on either straight gasoline or any combination of gasohol blends (gasoline mixed with alcohol). The fuel injection and engine timing are adjusted automatically according to what the percentage of alcohol the computer senses is in the fuel tank. Essentially, this is a gasoline vehicle with an electronic module usually mounted just outside the fuel tank to determine the percentage of alcohol in the blend.

C. Compressed Natural Gas
Compressed Natural Gas (CNG) is a fuel system where the CNG is stored in tanks as a gas not a liquid. Special precaution should be exercised if working with a fuel tank that has fuel in it.

Currently, there are three pressure platforms in use with CNG vehicles: 2,400 psi, 3,000 psi, and 3,600 psi. All of these have the potential to maim or cause injury. Do not open any fuel lines until the manual main shut-off valve has been closed. Consult vehicle engineering data for fuel manifold line layout.

CNG is a popular fuel because the gas enters the engine as a gas not an air/fuel mixture where there are tiny droplets of gasoline entering the combustion chamber. CNG will mix with oxygen more readily and burn much cleaner than gasoline.

D. Liquid Natural Gas
Liquid Natural Gas (LNG) has the same composition as CNG. However, it has been condensed down into liquid form. Propane is similar to LNG. The typical operating pressure is approximately 75 psi for most operating platforms. The most significant difference between a propane powered vehicle and an LNG/CNG vehicle is that propane is heavier than air. Methane (natural gas) is lighter than air. If there is a rupture in the fuel tank, propane will hang near the ground in a cloud, whereas methane will rise and dissipate. The presence of wind in both failure modes will aid in clearing the air of any flammable elements. The wind

will mix with the gas molecules and dilute the mix until it is no longer flammable.

One of the principal safety advantages of both CNG and LNG is that neither will auto ignite readily. Auto igniton of either CNG or LNG requires a surface temperature of approximately 1,300–1,400°F. In simpler terms, the exhaust system must be glowing red hot before either liquid or vaporous natural gas will auto ignite. If either type of gas leaks in the vicinity of the exhaust system on a vehicle, normal operating temperatures will not be hot enough to cause auto ignition unless there were some abnormal operating condition.

One of the safety features on modern OBD II fuel systems is that the system is programmed to go into Limited Operation Safety (LOS) mode if it detects an operating condition that will allow catalytic converter destruction. LOS mode will allow the vehicle to drive slowly off to the side. Normal operational performance is severely limited.

As a general rule, a leaking fuel system is not a serious fire hazard on an operating engine unless there is an open spark available to ignite the leaking gas. One problem is that LNG gas is heavier than air until it vaporizes. If a tank were leaking, there would be a flammable fog accumulated or emanating from the leak. Ambient temperatures will convert the LNG to an airborne state allowing it to rise and dispurse with any wind. CNG is lighter than air and disperses more easily into the atmosphere.

Both CNG and LNG vehicles can be readily identified. Federal Motor Vehicle Safety Standards Numbers 303 and 304 apply.

FMVSS 303 became effective in 1995. It deals with design safety on all systems outside the CNG or LNG fuel tank. The code applies to all vehicles sold in the U.S. market weighing less than 10,000 lbs. gross. The code also applies to school buses that weigh more than 10,000 lbs. gross. The most important part of this code is the requirement that the tank or vehicle be labeled with the familiar blue diamond with white letters identifying which type of fuel the vehicle operates on.

FMVSS 304 also became effective in 1995. This safety standard deals with the design of the CNG and LNG fuel tank itself. This code established four types of CNG and LNG fuel tanks:

Type One: This is a conventional all-metal tank.
Type Two: A conventional metal tank that is "hoop wrapped" with composite hoops.
Type Three: A metal liner surrounded completely by a composite exterior.
Type Four: An all-composite tank.

The current trend in CNG and LNG is expanding at an exponential rate. Engine designers prefer the CNG or LNG engine for several reasons: The gas mileage is better, the engines run cleaner, the bearings do not wear like gasoline engines, and the octane of CNG is approximately 120–130 RMS average. With good maintenance, a CNG or LNG engine could potentially deliver double the total service miles before overhaul is required as compared to a similar gasoline engine.

For the purposes of automotive fire analysis, the CNG or LNG engine differs only in the fact that it is next to impossible for a fuel leak to auto ignite on a hot exhaust. However, if the vehicle fire becomes hot enough, all the tank types have venting systems. If a fire occurs underneath one of these fuel tanks, it is not unusual to see the safety relief valve blown completely off of the tank or operating to vent the gas fuel.

E. Gas-electric hybrid vehicles

The hybrid power plant is increasing in popularity. These units are equipped with a conventional gasoline engine and an electric motor built into the flywheel housing. The flywheel and torque converter are constructed similar to their non-hybrid counterparts only with an electric motor built into the assembly. Thus, when the unit is in electric mode the crankshaft and transmission input shaft are being turned by the electric motor.

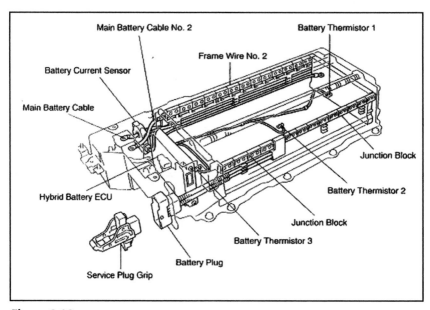

Figure 3.32

Some hybrid designs will utilize a gasoline engine that turns an alternator at a given RPM. Instead of an electric motor built into an extended flywheel housing, the design will locate an electric motor at one to four of the wheels. The alternator charges a battery that drives the electric motors. This design is similar to how diesel/electric locomotives operate.

A third design is a fully electric hybrid that runs on battery power alone. This model must be plugged in to recharge. Most models of this type have a limited range of 60-90 miles before a recharge is required.

The electric motors operate on AC. Most designs utilize a series-wound motor design. Thus, the RPM of the electric motor is dictated by the load applied. To power the electric motor there is a large battery pack typically located between the rear wheels. It is placed in this area because this is the safest area in a vehicle to resist crushing in a collision. Usually, the tires will break traction and the vehicle will be pushed away from the impacting vehicle long before any damage from crush can occur to the battery pack.

Most hybrids operate between 125–300 volts DC. The battery pack is constructed of numerous battery cells that are all hooked up in series. As a safety measure, there are "latching" relays that connect the battery to the battery cables inside the battery box. Typically, there is one latching relay for the positive side and one for the negative side. The latching relays are controlled by the normal 12-volt DC engine battery. The investigator should be certain the 12-volt DC engine battery is disconnected before performing an inspection on any hybrid. There are also some back-up safety measures mounted in the battery box in the form of thermistors to determine if the battery is getting too hot, and an inductive amperage coil to determine if too much current is in the circuit. Either condition will signal a computer module, also mounted inside the battery box, and the high voltage will be cut off automatically.

The hybrid system should be approached with *extreme caution* until the investigating engineer is positive that the high voltage battery is disabled. Contact with the positive and negative connectors may result in injury or death. These cables are isolated from the vehicle body ground. In addition to disconnecting the 12 volt engine battery to disable the high voltage battery, manufacturers will typically build a safety switch into the battery pack housing. See Figure 3.32 for a generic parts blow-up of the battery components inside a high voltage battery box.

If there is leakage present at NiMH (nickel metal hydrate) high voltage battery box, then the alkaline from the ruptured cells can be neutralized using a mixture of common boric acid and water. The alkaline from a ruptured cell can burn the skin or cause other injury if exposed. Use of gloves is highly recommended in approaching a NiMH-type battery.

Figure 3.33 *2007 Toyota Prius fire.*

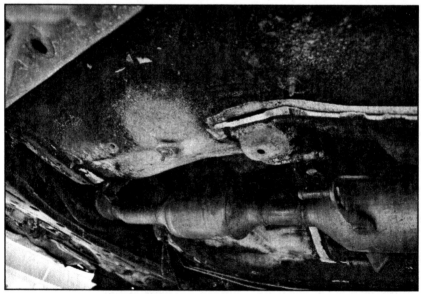

Figure 3.34 *2007 Toyota Prius fire.*

A second type of hybrid battery on the market is the lithium-ion (Li) battery. Li batteries utilize battery components that contain Li molecules. An Li battery can be partially discharged then recharged multiple times with no adverse effect. However, Li batteries present a greater fire hazard from internal failure than a NiMH battery. When a failure mode occurs, the Li molecules will generate oxygen internally as the thermal event progresses. One failing cell can generate sufficient heat to affect the next cell in what is termed a "cascading thermal event."

Regardless of battery type or configuration, the DC voltage platforms configured into hybrid vehicles is lethal. Proper training on how to disarm the high-voltage battery is essential to the investigating engineer or CFI.

Currently, the high voltage wiring is uniformly colored orange by all manufacturers in the U.S. market. Both the positive and negative wires will exit the high voltage battery box, route underneath the vehicle, then terminate at the inverter typically located on top of the gasoline engine. The inverter will change the DC electricity from the high voltage battery into AC electricity that the electric motor can use to turn the crankshaft. All of the high voltage wiring is completely insulated from the vehicle chassis. The high voltage negative side does not utilize the frame, body, or chassis of the hybrid to conduct electricity. The circuit is both isolated and dedicated by design.

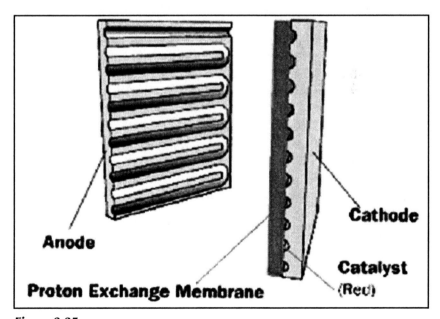

Figure 3.35

Thus, if either the high voltage positive or negative cable were to touch the vehicle chassis, nothing disastrous would occur. However, if the high voltage positive cable were to form a high-resistance short into the high voltage negative cable, this would present an excellent chance of starting an electrical fire. A dead short between the high voltage positive and negative cables would cause the inductive ammeter coils to sense a high drain. The battery control module should react by releasing the "latching" relays which cuts the power off before a fire can start. However, since a dead short will cause a tremendous amount of heat at the short and at the source, this creates the potential for the latching relays to "weld" their contacts together. If this occurs, the automatic safety systems built into the high voltage battery pack are rendered ineffective. The safety switch or service "grip" must be thrown or pulled to ensure there is no high voltage present so that fire investigation can proceed safely.

Figures 3.33 and 3.34 depict a dead short that occurred in the high voltage hybrid cables of a 2007 Toyota Prius. The cables are routed under the vehicle floor from the rear battery pack up to the engine inverter along the left frame rail. In this figure, note the large electrical arc damage across the underside of the vehicle on the driver's side.

The plug-in charge system is another device making its way onto hybrid vehicles. Hybrid models equipped with this feature can plug the high voltage battery in at night. This runs the battery charge up to higher than the 80 percent charge limit imposed by most manufacturers. With a fully charged high voltage battery, the average hybrid vehicle can run for approximately 25 miles before the gas engine will start. Normally, the computer module inside the high voltage battery pack will keep the battery charge between 20–80 percent (i.e., the battery is not allowed to run completely dead or completely charged). By conditioning the battery in this manner, it will add to battery lifetime.

A hybrid should be inspected carefully for signs of electrical overheat. A high voltage battery unit is quite powerful. When a failure has occurred internal to the battery unit, large arc beading is usually present. There can also be some small holes melted in the sheet metal of the body at the site of the shorting. Possibly, long lengths of copper cable appear as melted pools much like solder dripping from a soldering iron, except the droplets will be copper not lead.

F. Fuel cell vehicles

Although fuel cell vehicles are decades off from being available commercially, the technology to construct a working vehicle from a fuel cell is currently here. The main problems with the system are the lack of availability of hydrogen filling stations to fuel the process, the difficulty and expense involved in extracting liquid hydrogen, the fact that the fuel cell does not work well in cold climates, and the fact that fuel cells are fragile. This is not to mention the cost involved in replacing a fuel cell. Thus, the system can be operated only in moderate climates and currently cannot withstand the pounding to which the average consumer subjects their vehicle. Figure 3.35 is an example of a fuel cell.

The hydrogen and oxygen are supplied through tubes in cathode and anode assemblies, respectively. The cathode and anode are separated by an electron membrane. When hydrogen is pumped into one side of the tubes, oxygen into the other side of the tubes, and heat is applied, the end result is the production of voltage. The fuel cells are arranged in batteries that are wired in series much like a hybrid. The fuel cell battery is then connected to an electric motor to turn the wheels.

The main advantage of the fuel cell is the almost zero emissions, and if such a system becomes commercially feasible, this could drastically reduce our dependence on foreign oil.

Insufficient data exists on analyzing fuel cell vehicle fires as of the date of this printing (2013).

G. Lithium-ion batteries

A lithium-ion battery (secondary type) is different than a lithium battery (primary). Primary batteries are designed to be disposable not rechargeable. The most common lithium battery design uses metallic lithium as an anode and manganese dioxide as a cathode with a salt of lithium dissolved in an organic solvent.

By contrast the lithium-ion battery is designed to be recharged. The lithium-ions will move from the anode (negative) to the cathode (positive) during discharge, and back when charging. Unlike the primary lithium battery, the lithium-ion cell uses an intercalated lithium compound in the electrode material instead of metallic lithium.

There are two common construction types of lithium-ion batteries: first, a rolled-up version in a rigid tube. This design uses a negative electrode of graphite, a positive of metal oxide, with the electrolyte containing a lithium-ion salt suspended in an organic solvent.

The second design is most commonly flat cells that embed the lithium-ions into a plasticizer gel. This design can also be rolled into a rigid tube. The most common types of plasticizer gel used are polyethylene oxide or polyacrylonitrile. The gel-type of configuration will contain greater amounts of anions and cations because the lithium-ions have been ground into finer *nanoparticles*. This creates greater surface area for the electrons to affix during a charge. A greater quantity of anions and cations in the electrolyte will allow for a higher ampere-hour rating.

Lithium-ion batteries are prone to failure leading to fire. Most commonly, the failure mode will be while the unit is being charged. The battery pack will begin to degrade over time. The electrolyte wears down causing the battery to discharge in a shorter period of time and produce less amperage. The consumer will typically have complaints about shortened range of the hybrid vehicle.

A lithium ion battery is comprised from a material containing lithium ions. Both the cathode and the anode are comprised from materials that contain lithium ions. There are differing materials used to construct a lithium ion battery. Graphite and copper are the most popular materials used to construct the anode. The cathode is commonly constructed from one of the following materials: lithium cobalt oxide, lithium iron phosphate, lithium manganese oxide, manganese spinel, and some other proprietary formulas. Titanium disulfide was common in earlier designs, although titanium cathodes are still found in use today.[39–41]

The development of iron-phosphate *nanoparticles* less than 100 nanometers in width allowed for greater density of the lithium ions. This greatly increases the capacity of the lithium ion design by increasing the available surface area of the electrode.

Sony Corp® was the first to develop and release a commercially feasible lithium ion battery in 1991.[42] These batteries used lithium cobalt oxide rolled in layers. This development revolutionized consumer electronic products. The main advantages of the design are size, portability, light weight-to-energy ratio, high

Figure 3.36 X-ray of lithium-ion battery with intact fuse discs.

Figure 3.37 Exploded lithium-ion battery unrolled.

energy density, and an exceptional cycling life. Another advantage of lithium ion batteries is that they do not suffer the "memory" effect common to other rechargeable battery designs.

The lithium ion battery will lose capacity based simply on its age. From the day the lithium ion "slurry" was spread out on the insulator and formed into a cell, the material will begin to lose capacity. The internal resistance of the lithium ion battery rises with age. The capacity of the battery deteriorates over time not duty cycles. This fact is not widely published. However, as the capacity decreases over time, the time required to recharge that cell is similarly diminished and decreases proportionately.

The presence of a circuit monitor as a safety device in "smart" lithium ion batteries will, by design, lose battery charge at a greater rate because the monitor circuit will draw a tiny amount of current to run the device. Thus, a "smart" lithium ion battery will lose its charge sooner than a "dumb" one. As a general rule, the circuit monitor in a lithium ion battery pack will be found somewhere inside the plastic casing of the battery pack. "Smart" lithium ion batteries will self-discharge at a rate of approximately 5 percent per month due to the circuit monitor draw.

Batteries are not compatible with extreme temperatures. An exception to this rule is thermal batteries, which are rare and are generally only found in military applications. If a lithium ion battery is exposed to repeated high charge rates and/or high operating temperatures, this will dramatically reduce its lifetime.

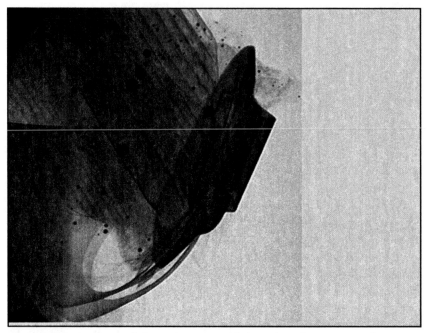

Figure 3.38 *X-ray of a lithium battery with fuse disc shorting out the battery.*

1. Failure modes

Lithium ion batteries have several safety features found on the different designs.[41] These include:

- Shut Down Separator. This is something like a fuse usually built into the top of the battery for high heat circuit separation. Its physical appearance is like one or more small disc(s) near the cathode. Figure 3.36 depicts a normal shut down separator.
- Pressure Relief Vent. The most common lithium ion cell design is a metal tube with the "jelly roll" of lithium ion slurry, a layered oxide metal tube for the cathode, and a proprietary material for the anode. The "jelly roll" is rolled up and stuffed into the metal tube. The Pressure Relief Vent is a small hole(s) in the tube. The "jelly roll" can also be configured into flat plates.
- Tear Away Tab. This tab interrupts the circuit when high internal pressure causes the "jelly roll" to blow out of the metal tube.
- Thermal Interrupt. This device is used to prevent overcurrent/overcharging damage.

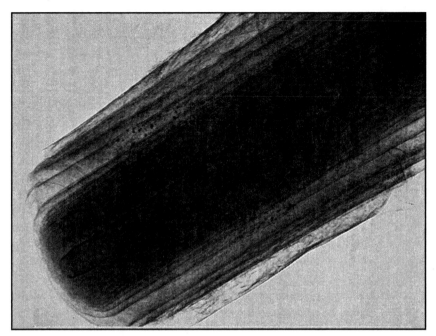

Figure 3.39 *X-ray of exploded lithium-ion battery.*

Lithium ion batteries can ignite, rupture, or explode when exposed to high temperature environments or develop an internal short. The general failure modes can typically be traced to one or more of the following:

1) Torn or ripped insulator. This can occur if the metal bits used in the lithium ion "slurry" are too large. The large bits of metal can poke through the insulator that is compromising it, causing an internal short on the cell. The insulator could also be defective from the manufacturing process. See Figure 3.37.

2) High temperature or unventilated charge mode. For example, if a lithium ion battery is charged in direct sunlight on a hot day sitting on the dashboard of a car, this can cause high internal pressures. As noted, high temperatures reduce performance and the life span dramatically.

3) Overcharging. All batteries must be charged at a slightly higher voltage than their rated output. This includes lithium ion batteries. A high internal heat can cause the shut down separator to melt. This device looks like a small disc at the cathode end of the battery inside the battery cell casing. If the device works as designed, circuit voltage is interrupted. One common failure mode of the separator device is if it melts away

from the cathode pin but drops down in a crooked manner or warps inside the battery. This can turn the separator device into a metal disc that is now shorting the battery out internally. See Figure 3.38. Overcharging over time can also compromise the insulator via excessive heat.

Any time a lithium ion battery enters any overheat or other failure mode, it is not uncommon for the battery pack to suffer a cascading thermal failure of one or more of the other cells. Investigative steps to follow and signs to look for to determine the primary failed part include:

- Locate the remains of all the cells to make the total cell count of the battery pack correct. If not immediately discovered, keep looking. Even when a cell explodes, most of the contents of the cell are intact somewhere in the fire debris nearby the site of failure.
- Package up all battery cell evidence into separate evidence bags. A useful tool here to inspect the interior of the "jelly roll" is to use a real time x-ray machine at a local testing laboratory. Look for signs of internal splatter, melted metal, or compromised insulator material. Figure 3.39 depicts an X-ray of an exploded lithium ion battery.
- After all cells are located, and the decision whether or not to x-ray the evidence first has been agreed upon, then open the metal casing of each cell very carefully using a small pair of wire cutters. Remove the "jelly roll." The overheated cell will have holes in the anode and the insulator. The lithium ion "slurry" is usually crumbled.
- Look for signs of high electrical heat. This includes exploded cells, cells that show discoloration on their metal casing that cannot be attributed to convective heat from the flaming combustibles, and cells that have blown the "jelly roll" out of the tube casing.
- When all of the cells have been cut open and the "jelly roll" removed from each, then unroll each of the cells taking care to organize the tubes with their contents. Measure the average length of the anode from each cell. The failed cells will commonly have holes and discoloration from electrical heat; the anode will be considerably shorter than the others; and/or the cathode is fused to the anode (i.e., you cannot unroll part of the anode because it is fused or pieces of the anode broke off during the thermal release event).

Obviously from the discussion, there is excess oxygen available at the cathode during a failure mode. If a lithium ion battery develops a heavy short internally, this can lead to converting all of the energy in the cell into heat in an oxidizing exothermic reaction. A heavy internal short can raise the temperature of the battery to several hundred degrees Fahrenheit in a fraction of a second.

However, the sudden high heat resulting from the collapse of the electrical charge is not what causes the typical fire in a lithium ion battery. Rather, the failure mode is more commonly a high resistance short-to-ground causing a gradual thermal increase internal to the affected cell. Typically, the failure mode that leads to catastrophic failure and fire will occur during battery recharging. The cell bursts apart from the accumulation of oxygen greater than the cell vent can outgas. When the cell finally bursts apart, then heat has likely accumulated in the immediate area to potentially cause ignition of localized combustibles. The internal heat can also build to the point of auto ignition of the cell plastic itself that groups the cells into a battery pack. Finally, the failure mode may very well involve the wire from the transformer charging the battery pack.

When a battery pack has developed an internal short in one of the cells, failure mode leading to fire *during* use is not common. The battery charge merely runs down sooner. However, fire from a shorted battery pack in use is not an unheard-of phenomenon. Battery fire during a period of non-use is generally limited to high capacity batteries (i.e., something with the capacity of a car lead acid battery).

Regardless, the typical failure mode pattern occurs when the battery pack is being recharged. One or more cells have developed a slight internal failure mode such as a compromised insulator. Heat begins to build at the site of compromise; the battery charger continues to charge the battery pack, causing heat to build, oxygen is released into the battery tube as the electrolyte synthesizes. Finally, internal heat continues to build until a sudden thermal energy release event occurs.

The cells are often made in a different country than where the battery is constructed using these cells. The plastic may well be constructed from a formula that has higher Volatile Organic Compounds (VOCs) than allowable for sale in the U.S. market. This creates a product that can catch fire easier and propagate fire faster than one designed to the correct U.S. standards. Product content determination is crucial to any fire investigation.

For example, what is the course of action if the investigation reveals that the manufacturer willfully and knowingly built the battery casing from plastic that was highly flammable and banned in the U.S.? How is the focus of the investigation affected if a fatality from the fire is involved compared to only a property loss?

Clearly, this part of the fire investigation should be given proper consideration. One method is to procure an exemplar battery pack, de-construct it, and have the materials tested. Sometimes, there is a code cast into the plastic part that can be used to determine the composition of the material.

Figure 3.40 New style SRS module. No moving parts.

Figure 3.41 Old style SRS module. Screwdriver is moving weighted roller against a spring coiled around it.

A battery cell or battery pack that was *not* the primary failed part but just happened to be sitting at or near the area of origin will show convective heat damage from the outside moving inward.

As the consumer electronic device or charging battery pack (external charging system) is carefully de-layered, inspect the plastic pieces as they begin to break off. If the greatest amount of heat damage is found on the inside of the pieces, then a determination has been be made with 100 percent certainty that the battery pack was the source of the fire not a victim.

As with most electrical fires, the primary failed part is usually destroyed. This was the area the fire burned the longest. However, understanding the mechanism for failure within the battery pack assembly and the chemical reactions that occur for a lithium ion battery to operate are essential to the technical expert in deposition or trial testimony.

In conclusion, the best method to determine the primary failed part is to have a complete understanding of the circuitry, safety features commonly found, the chemistry involved, and failure mode signs. Remember, most engineers that work for manufacturers are trained that a) their product is never at fault, and b) if you cannot win by logical technical argument, then obfuscate. Muddy the waters a bit. However, this strategy only succeeds when the judge or jury are not properly educated by the technical expert.

H. Supplemental restraint systems and Event Data Recorders

Supplemental restraint systems (SRS) are commonly called "airbags." Driver side airbags were originally an option. Vehicles manufactured for sale in the U.S. market were required to have dual frontal airbags after September 1, 1996. Seatbelts and SRS airbags are required per FMVSS 208.

The first Crash Data Recorders (CDR) began appearing in the late 1980s and early 1990s. The term has since modified to "Event Data Recorder" (EDR) in the vernacular of most manufacturers. General Motors and Chrysler were among the first to equip some of their models with an EDR.

The first designs only recorded 5-second intervals. As computer memory became less expensive, the timeframe recorded and the type of data collected increased. The more advanced designs with give a timeframe window of 15 seconds or longer are now more common.

The EDR is built into the SRS module. The SRS module functions to deploy the airbags and record collision data. The type of memory used is "Program Read Only Memory" (PROM). If the airbags are deployed, the crash data timeframe will be locked into permanent memory even if power is lost. Figure 3.40 depicts a modern SRS module with an EDR built into the SRS circuit board.

If a collision occurs but the airbags do not deploy, then the EDR will merely record over the top of the old data as soon as power is restored and the ignition key is turned on. The old data will be lost. One feature that may be recorded and retained is if one of the "discriminating" sensors were to trip or signal that a sudden deceleration occurred.

SRS systems commonly utilize two types of sensors to deploy an airbag: Discriminating sensors and a "safing" switch. The discriminating sensor may be mounted outside the SRS module. If so configured, there will commonly be a sensor mounted to the core support or front frame. These will universally have either a yellow convolute conduit or a yellow connector. The discriminating sensor may also be mounted inside the SRS module.

The discriminating sensor will signal that a sudden deceleration (collision) has occurred. The second type of sensor in the SRS system is called a "safing" switch. The safing switch will make the final connection required to deploy current to the exploding squibs.

It is possible in minor collisions for the discriminating sensor to signal a sudden deceleration event is occurring. The safing switch will make the final determination that the sudden deceleration is or is not of significant magnitude to allow the airbags to deploy.

If the discriminating sensor in an EDR-equipped SRS system signals a sudden deceleration event is occurring but the safing switch determines the event lacks sufficient magnitude to deploy the airbags, then the EDR will record that the discriminating sensor has sent a signal. This indication will remain in the EDR memory for anywhere up to approximately 240 cycles of the ignition switch. The memory will then erase that the event occurred.

Older SRS systems utilized mechanical sensors. These designs included ball bearings held by spring-loaded "claws" and cylindrical rollers with flat springs wrapped around them. Figure 3.41 depicts an older SRS module with a mechanical safing switch. The small screwdriver is holding the rolling cylinder off its base slightly. If the collision were of sufficient force to dislodge the ball or for the roller cylinder to overcome the spring, then the ball or cylinder would make contact at the end of its travel to create the circuit that deploys the airbags. If the impact were of sufficient force but had an oblique angle of impact, this causes the spring-loaded cylinder to roll improperly down the channel. It will hang up on the sides preventing a deployment. These designs were phased out starting in the mid-1990s.

Also commonly found in SRS modules are capacitor(s). Some designs will employ a larger single capacitor or connect several capacitors in series to increase the available voltage in the airbag circuit. Thus, if the car battery were to be disabled in the first part of the collision event, the SRS module will maintain sufficient electrical charge in the capacitors to allow the airbag squibs to explode. In short, the SRS module does not need the car battery to deploy the airbags. Most designs will allow the SRS module to maintain power required for airbag deployment for at least 90 seconds.

Newer SRS modules designs incorporate "accelerometers." These sensors react to force the nanosecond force is applied. They are used as discriminating sensors, in the safing switch, and to record the deceleration time and speed into the EDR.

Most SRS systems will operate on a 10–25 millisecond "window" for the system to "wake up" and make a determination that a sudden deceleration event of significant force is occurring. If parameters are met, the SRS module will send a signal to the exploding squibs to deploy the airbags within 35 milliseconds. Thus, the system has fully inflated the airbags within 35 milliseconds.

Most SRS designs require an impact occurs within 30° either way of center-line of travel (total 60°).

What the system seeks is a moderate or greater collision that is going to cause the driver's head to strike the horn pad directly.

The airbags should not deploy if the collision angle is oblique. Additionally, the SRS airbags should not deploy on a rollover collision. If the collision event is causing the driver's head to aim toward the stereo then airbag deployment may cause serious injury or death by breaking the driver's neck. Thus, the SRS module must determine both force and vector angle to allow the deployment signal to leave the SRS module via the safing switch.

The exploding squibs are a small thimble containing a compound called "sodium azide." This compound will explode if exposed to electrical current, compression, or fire. Basically, an airbag is a small bomb waiting to explode in the driver's face.

Earlier systems were configured with a single exploding squib in each air-bag module. This design will inflate the airbag at approximately 200 mph. These designs have more potential for occupant injury than the new "smart" airbag systems. The newer designs will have two exploding squibs per airbag module. The total sodium azide charge is divided in half. The safing switch makes the decision to deploy one squib on moderate collisions of approximately 12 mph and both squibs on higher collisions of 18+ mph.

SRS system components will include the frontal airbags, side "curtain" airbags, side "thorax protection" airbags, and seatbelt "pre-tensioner" exploding squibs.

Frontal airbags will deploy from the horn pad and dashboard. Most designs will incorporate a passenger seat occupant sensor. Some advanced occupant de-signs are capable of determining the general size of the occupant. The deploy-ment strategy will adapt to the smaller individual. Some passenger frontal airbags will inflate upwards then push off the windshield into the passenger area. These designs invariably break the windshield.

Side "curtain" airbags are a long airbag that will cover the roofline area from the front seats to the rear seats. These commonly utilize compressed air to inflate. An exploding squib is mounted to an air cylinder that provides the compressed air to inflate the airbag. This design will provide occupant head protection from colliding with the side windows and pillars.

Side "thorax protection" airbag designs commonly are mounted inside the front seats. The side airbag will explode out from specialized stitching in the side of the front seats. This type of airbag provides driver or passenger protection from the hip to the top of the shoulders.

"Pre-tensioner" seatbelts have two common designs: One incorporates an exploding squib inside the female buckle portion. When deployed, the exploding squib propels a piston rearward inside a cylinder. Attached to the piston is a cable. The other end of the cable is anchored to the female portion of the seatbelt buckle. When deployed, this design yanks downward on the female portion of the seat belt causing it to lock up on the spooler.

The second type of "pre-tensioner" seatbelt will locate the exploding squib in the seatbelt spooler assembly. This type of design locks the seatbelt from retracting or spooling outward when deployed.

The "pre-tensioner" seatbelt designs should deploy when the frontal airbags deploy.

There are newer "smart" designs that are currently not sold in the U.S. market except in certain limited high-line vehicles. These designs will monitor occupant position. If the occupant moves into a position whereby the airbags may injure the occupant, the SRS module "senses" the change in position and cancels operation of the airbag that may injure the occupant.

For example, a passenger is looking into the glove box for something. They have shifted their torso forward toward the dashboard and the head is looking down into the glove box. Or, the passenger has put their feet up on top of the dashboard. Should the passenger frontal airbag deploy in either of these conditions, serious injury may result. As soon as the occupant returns to normal seating position, the airbag resumes normal "ready" status.

One fact about SRS systems that is not widely published is that the exploding squibs have a shelf life. The exploding squib modules are designed for a 10-year lifespan. It is possible that the exploding squibs may not be compromised after a 10-year operation cycle. However, it is possible for moisture ingress into the exploding squib. Should the sodium azide absorb moisture, it may not explode as designed. Partial or non-deployment much like a wet firecracker can occur.

I. Golf cart fires

1. Gas-powered golf carts

Golf carts are defined as an "amusement ride" by most states. This is the legal definition even though golf carts are allowed to drive over designated public roadways in many communities. None of the models currently on the market support the legal definition of an automobile. Some models are marketed as "Golf Cars" because the body resembles a production automobile. Regardless, they are not automobiles. The biggest issues present when one catches fire that spreads to a structure.

Some features will be commonly found on all makes and models of golf carts. For example, the brake system most commonly found is a mechanical link rod that routes to each rear wheel. When the driver depresses the brake pedal, this pulls on the rod that in turn pulls on a cam in the rear brakes. The cam will spread the brake shoes out against the rotating drum. As a general rule, golf carts only have rear brakes not front ones.

One exception would be off-road utility carts that are used for off-road recreation or for farm use. These units will commonly go faster and traverse steeper terrain than will golf carts. The investigating engineer may find a hydraulic brake system equipped on such models.

The most common steering systems configured on golf carts are a tiller handle for three-wheel designs and rack-and-pinion steering for four-wheel models.

One curious design factor that is common in both three- and four-wheel designs that are configured with a top is that the unit can rollover much easier when the steering has turned the wheels all the way one direction or the other.

If the golf cart has rolled over as a prelude to the onset of fire, then the investigating engineer should procure a similar model and test the propensity for rollover. Set up an appropriate test jig to pull the golf cart over in a manner imitating the actual unit that rolled over then caught fire. Include a tension meter as part of the testing. Assemble three or four strong men. With the steering wheels straight ahead, test the golf cart for the amount of force required to bring the unit to its balance point just before it rolls on its side. Pull from the right side. Next, test the left side.

After a wheels-straight test is performed, then turn the wheels all the way to the left. Repeat the test. Next, turn the wheels all the way to the right. Repeat the test. Compare the results. It is common to see upwards of a 30 percent difference in the force required to cause the unit to rollover when the wheels are fully turned to the left or right. The report should reflect the figures obtained through the rollover testing.

Since golf carts are not automobiles, they are not equipped with the sophisticated smog equipment or catalytic converters commonly found on cars, trucks, and newer motorcycles. However, some states *may* require installation of a catalytic converter. The investigating engineer should check the laws of the state the loss occurred in. The question is "was the golf cart sold in compliance with the state laws?" There is always the possibility the golf cart was imported to the state from another where the laws are different.

The body on golf carts will commonly be comprised of fiberglass. Many times, the fiberglass is modified by the addition of Olefin or Polyolefin oils. Both of these act as a weatherproofing agent to resist UV exposure. The presence of these oils in the fiberglass will enhance the ability of the fiberglass to burn and support flaming combustion.

A second confounding factor is that most golf carts will be equipped with a vinyl seat that is built onto a piece of plywood. The sun top will also commonly be comprised of vinyl. There may even be a plexiglass windshield. The plywood for the seat will burn hot and cause a good deal of damage to the other components making analysis that much more difficult.

Gas-powered golf carts will commonly be equipped with a stop/start feature. This feature may be configured in addition to a standard starter motor. When the golf cart comes to a stop, the engine dies out. When the driver depresses the accelerator pedal, the engine starts again. The golf cart will commonly be configured with a starter/alternator (or generator) built into the same unit. This same stop/start technology is what gives hybrid cars the biggest boost in gas mileage.

The failure modes leading to fire on a gas-powered golf cart are the same as automobile fires. This includes electrical fire and gas leak fire. However, most golf carts are direct drive without power steering. This eliminates a transmission fluid leak or power steering leak coming in contact with a hot exhaust.

If the gasoline leaks with the golf cart running, the establishment of fire requires that the fumes from the leaking gasoline find their way to an ignition source. Of course, this will be an operational mode fire. If fire occurs more than approximately 10-15 minutes (or less depending on ambient air temperature) after engine shut down, then auto ignition is not possible. If gas leaking then igniting is suspected for a golf cart stored in a garage, then the ignition source should be identified. An example might be a water heater located in the same garage as the golf cart that is leaking gasoline.

Electrical fire is the other type of fire common to gas-powered golf carts. Most commonly, the gas-powered golf cart will be configured with a 12-volt DC battery. The investigating engineer or CFI must identify the accessories that were added after the golf cart left the factory. Many times owners will install headlamps, air fans, decorative lights, stereos, etc. as optional accessories. The investigating engineer or CFI must eliminate all aftermarket options as causal factors in the fire.

Failure to examine and eliminate the accessories that were not OEM equipped will not be missed by factory engineers during a fire investigation. The training factory engineers receive dictates that the options must be eliminated first before focusing on factory-configured components as being the primary failed part that caused the fire.

Since there are many different configurations of golf carts, the investigating engineer or CFI should procure both the Service Workshop Manual and the Parts Manual. Many times, the Service Workshop Manual information will contain what is needed for the investigation report. Also, many times the Parts Manual will contain a useful physical layout architectural drawing of the subject golf cart. These will assist the investigative report with accuracy of parts layout and system operation.

2. Electric golf carts

An electric golf cart will be powered by a battery pack. The common platforms these units operate on are 24-volt, 36-volt, 48-volt, and 72-volt. Of the different platforms available, the 36- and 48-volt systems are the most common.

The batteries found on most golf carts are termed "deep cycle" batteries. Most are lead-acid in construction. A deep-cycle battery is designed to be charged, run dead, then be re-charged again without the same accelerated sulfiding that occurs to the battery plates. The sulfiding reaction will occur but over a slower period of time. This is due to the battery manufacturer utilizing an alloy of lead with cadmium or antimony to create a harder battery plate. For example, if a common automotive "cranking" battery is used in a golf cart, the battery's construction will cause it to fail in about 6-8 months when placed in golf cart applications where the batteries are being drawn to a state of full discharge regularly. A deep cycle battery will put up with this application use for a much longer period of time.

One item the investigating engineer and CFI should be aware of is the configuration of the batteries used. Some manufacturers will utilize an 8-volt DC battery in place of the 12-volt configuration. Sometimes, 6-volt batteries will be found. The investigating tip here is to make sure the battery voltage is correct for the system. Count the cell holes or cell grouping of the batteries. Lead-acid batteries will produce 2.1 volts per cell. Add up the cells to equal the output of the battery.

Electric golf carts will be commonly be equipped with a forward and reverse switch. This switch can be mounted anywhere on the cart that is within reach of the driver. There will also be some type of switch in the accelerator pedal assembly. The micro-switch will close its contacts to inform the controller that the driver wishes the car to go forward or reverse. How much throttle is desired by the driver is determined by a variable resistor also mounted in the accelerator pedal assembly.

The next component that is common to electric golf carts is a large contactor unit. This unit will provide the high current and voltage to the motor. It will commonly be located nearby the electric motor. The contactor is powered by turning the ignition switch on. It works very similarly to a starter solenoid for a gasoline starter motor.

A big potential for electrical fire occurs when the large contactor "welds" its contacts together internally. This causes the electric motor controller to be powered up even when the golf cart ignition key is turned off.

The next component for discussion on electric golf carts is the motor controller. These units are fairly large. Most will have a "B+" terminal for battery positive, a "B-" for battery negative, and an "M" terminal for "Motor Positive." These three cable will be the largest ones that route to the controller.

There will be a number of other wires that also route to the controller that will be grouped in a connector. These will be input/output wires for the computer controller, to turn the logic circuit on, forward or reverse input, "tow" switch input, and to allow for "regenerative" and for "plug" braking.

Most controller units will have a removable plug that reveals a serial connector port. This connector is the one used by the factory and service personnel to adjust the settings of the controller via use of a "scanner" tool.

Regenerative braking is where the mass of the golf cart is driving the electric motor faster than the system is driving the motor. This downhill movement will cause the motor to generate electricity. The amount of electricity generated will be fed into the batteries to maintain the charge level.

Plug braking or "plugging" is a feature where the electric motor is used to brake the electric golf cart. If so equipped, the driver merely moves the forward/reverse switch to the reverse position without taking his or her foot off of the accelerator. This causes electrical reverse rotation within the electric drive motor. The golf cart should stop in a much shorter distance. This is an emergency feature that should not be routinely used to stop the golf cart.

The CFI or investigating engineer should interview the owner of the golf cart to determine if the owner is aware that a plug braking feature is equipped. If the owner is aware of this feature, then the question to resolve is how often the feature is engaged. If the owner is unaware of this feature, then overuse of the plug braking feature can be eliminated at the cause.

Many designs of electric golf carts will equip a computer module with a "field effect coil" built into the module. This component will perform two functions: The field effect coil will "read" the voltage present in the unit via "field effect" of the voltage and/or amperage. As the voltage drops, the module will signal the motor controller to cut back on the power. It is very possible the controller will drop into "Limited Operation Safety (LOS)" mode.

The LOS mode is a built-in feature that senses when an operating condition occurs that can damage the motor or controller, it will severely limit the performance of the golf cart. The driver will either drive it back to the golf course queue with a "no power" complaint, or the driver will summon a service company to fix the golf cart. The purpose of this feature is to protect the controller and motor by making the driver aware the unit has an operating issue.

The second purpose of the field effect coil performs is to determine if the ignition key is left in the "on" position. If the computer module detects the key has been left on, it will respond by disallowing the batteries to take a charge when connected to the charger.

The purpose of the "tow" switch is so that the electric golf cart can be dragged back to the service area without the electric motor generating current.

One thing the CFI or investigating engineer might find in the fire debris is a simple loop of metal around the B+ cable. Not all units will use this device. The loop is not connected to anything. It merely has a "smoothing" effect on the field effect that occurs with all electrical current. It will function to absorb spikes. This unit should not be confused with the field effect coil described above. Most commonly, the current smoothing loop will be around the B+ cable. The field effect coil will be mounted into the computer module. The B- cable will pass through the coil.

The controller unit on the electric golf cart is designed to protect itself and the golf cart from many failure modes. However, it cannot protect the golf cart from *all* failure modes that lead to fire.

Unfortunately, most golf carts have a fiberglass body. This will assist in destroying the fire evidence because fiberglass burns well and will provide excellent temperature transfer properties to the flaming combustion.

Some issues the investigating engineer or CFI should look into are any recent service that has been performed on the golf cart. Also, are there any open recalls for the model golf cart suspected? How many other golf carts of this design have caught fire?

As an example, a golf cart caught fire then the fire spread to the garage the golf cart was parked in. This is a witnessed fire where certainty is 100 percent that the golf cart itself started the fire. The investigating engineer or CFI investigation reveals that the wiring bundle that routes to the controller underneath the seat was crushed against the bulkhead causing a short that led to an electrical fire.

The repair orders for any recent work should be consulted to determine if the technician working on the golf cart somehow damaged the wiring bundle.

Perhaps the technician leaned on or sat on the wiring bundle while perform the service work; pinching or damaging the wiring causing the short that led to fire.

The investigative tip here is to leave no stone unturned. The investigating engineer or CFI should have a working knowledge of the technology involved on the golf cart. The attorneys representing the golf cart manufacturer will attempt to determine the skill level of the investigating engineer or CFI. If any weakness is perceived then this will make subrogation difficult if not impossible.

Chapter 4

Automotive Composites

4.1 Early Plastics

Plastic has gone from an early novelty material to being 10 percent of the total vehicle weight on modern vehicles. Early plastic composites manufactured for automotive use contained a high content of volatile organic compounds (VOCs). These can be aromatic (smells like new carpet) or embedded (no off-gassing). The early formulas were highly flammable. Many times the plastics were ignited by a carelessly discarded cigarette.

Automobile manufacturers have a difficult manufacturing constraint in the selection of plastic composites to be used in the interior of a vehicle: The plastics selected cannot off-gas so badly that a consumer is overcome by aromatic vapors when the windows are rolled up. However, there must be some off-gassing of plastic vapor to satisfy "that new car smell" desired by a new owner.

Over time, the manufacturers have developed plastic composite formulas which satisfy people's desire to own a new-smelling vehicle and are flame retardant. As discussed earlier, FMVSS 302 was initiated to make the flammability of interior materials resistant to cigarettes and matches. The spirit of the code was not to force the manufacturers to use totally fireproof materials, merely fire-resistant ones.

4.2 Thermoplastics and Thermosetting Plastics

Automotive plastics fall into three major categories: thermoplastics, thermosetting plastics and elastomers. The principle advantages of plastics in automobiles is the ability to shape plastics without machining.

A thermoplastic is one which will soften and can be reshaped with heat many times. Each time heat is applied to a certain degree the plastic material becomes workable until it cools. This effect can be somewhat reduced by using mixtures of thermoplastic polymers.

Thermosetting plastics are those plastics which are set under the influence of heat and pressure. They cannot be reheated and reworked. Thermoset plastics, once set, stay that way. These plastics will retain their dimensional stability up to temperatures almost as high as the processing temperature due to closely spaced cross-linking. Fillers are almost always added to thermosetting plastics to counteract their inherent brittleness.

An elastomer plastic has many useful applications because of its elasticity. The elasticity of this type of plastic is dependent on operation in moderate temperatures. To maintain elasticity of an elastomer plastic in a wide variety of climates, the material is vulcanized (widely-spaced cross-linking) to stabilize its molecular bonds.[5]

There is an easy way to test for the type of plastic being inspected. The sample can be slowly heated using a cigarette lighter. If the material softens and becomes workable then it is a thermoplastic. If the plastic begins to turn brown, black or burn and shrink away from the flame then it is a thermosetting material.

4.3 Olefins and Polyolefins

Olefins and polyolefins are plastics commonly found in earlier vehicle designs and entry-level vehicles. They are used primarily due to their low cost. All olefins have a high petroleum content. Hence, these types of automotive composites will support burning combustion better than other polymerics unless a non-flammable material is added as part of the overall composite.

There is a simple test the investigating engineer can perform in the field to determine if the material being inspected is an olefin. A piece of coarse sand paper such as 36–80 grit is used to sand the material. If the material sands cleanly producing dust, then the sample is a non-olefin. If the material being sanded smears or has a waxy look after sanding, it is most likely an olefin.

An olefin or polyolefin material can create a fairly hot fire with good transfer characteristics to the other materials located close to the fire. This mechanism may contribute to a hotter-than-normal-looking burn pattern. However, even when this occurs the burn pattern still does not resemble the heat release rate of an accelerant-based fire.

Olefins and polyolefins when added to a plastic increase the ability of that plastic to withstand ultraviolet rays and weathering better than plastics without olefins. However, when incorporated into the plastic, this will render out as a slightly more combustible VOC's than found in other polymerics.

4.4 Rubber and Rubber Components

Rubber and rubber components contain neoprene, carbon black, styrene, and polybutadiene as some of the major components. As a general rule, rubber is very difficult to ignite. However, once ignition has been achieved, rubber is difficult to extinguish. Rubber and rubber lattices are prone to supporting burning combustion.

Normally, tires will not be involved in an automobile fire unless the power steering fluid or gasoline has ignited one or more of the tires. However, should a tire ignite in a fire the heat release rate is spectacular. The burn pattern will also be dramatically affected due to the addition of such an accelerant to propagate the fire. A burning tire has the potential to impinge sufficient heat to melt copper wire. The wheelhouse of the vehicle can act to entrain the heated air from the burning tire into the engine compartment or cabin area. Most vehicles have splashguards around the inside of the wheelhouse. This material will add to the overall BTU load once it ignites. The investigating engineer may find pieces of the apron or firewall have been notched away to lighten the vehicle weight in modern designs.

A common tire fire is due to an axle fire on a heavy truck. However, axle fires can and do occur to automobiles. An axle fire is the usual result of descending a steep grade while the driver is riding the brake. The brakes overheat and ignite the oil and road grime residue accumulated on the backing plates of the brakes or axle. The fire spreads to the tire itself. This type of fire is particularly dangerous to spectators or firemen. A burning inflated tire can explode and send molten burning rubber outward. If any flaming or molten particles land on the skin or eyes, severe burns or blindness may result.

Normally, an axle fire will be limited to the wheel on which it occurred and the surrounding components. These types of fires lack the access to flammable hydrocarbons. The exception to this case is if one of the rear tires happens to burn the fuel filler neck through or spreads to a flammable liquid.

4.5 Polymerics and Nanocomposites

Polymeric composite materials consist of at least two physically or chemically different components. These components must be tightly bound together at a defined interface. The formation of the interface must not have a negative effect on any of the two bound components. Under these two conditions it is possible to bond many materials together. Composite materials exhibit combinations of properties which none of the components alone possesses. Different classes of composite materials are:

> **particle composite materials**. These are powder-filled resins, hard materials, plastic-bonded magnet, and cements.

laminated composite materials. These are composite or "sandwich" panels and resin-bonded fabric.

fiber composite materials. These are polymer bonded fibers such as fiberglass, Panox®, glass fibers, carbon-fiber, and cotton-fiber-reinforced plastics.

Polymeric composite and nanocomposite plastics make up some of the most fire-resistant plastics equipped on modern vehicles. Essentially, minerals and fibers such as mica, rock flour, glass fibers, glass chopped, Panox, talcum, calcium, and clay are tightly bonded to the polymeric composite or nanocomposite in quantities of up to 40 percent of total weight. This has the effect of reducing the *combustibility* of the material and raising the point of ignition. SAE Standard 1344 establishes classes of these nanocomposites which have the properties of "Self-Extinguishing/Not Burnable" and "Will Not Ignite." Part of the resistance of these materials to resist flammability is the highly cross-linked nature of their molecular structure.

Flammability behavior is the result of a complex set of factors; some of these are dictated by the material composition, others by the conditions of exposure. For a pure polymer, this behavior begins with the ability of its chemical bonds to resist heat-induced breakage. When a plastic object burns, it does so because heat from the flames (or elsewhere) is, in part, being transferred into the condensed phase and breaking off molecular fragments which oxidize in the gas phase to sustain the flames. Thus, the thermal stability of a polymer is more effectively able to reject the heat input from an adjacent flame because of the high surface temperature it achieves before degrading to volatile fragments. The structure of a polymer allows it to reradiate more of that heat to the surrounding environment. On the other extreme of heat exposure, the conditions of heat release rate may be such that the surroundings are not passive receivers of heat. Rather, they themselves may be hot or contain hot gasses capable of radiating heat to the polymer surface. This heat tends to counter the surface radiation loss from the polymer and enhance its flammability because it helps sustain the high temperatures which induce thermal degradation.

Figures 4.1 through 4.4 depict fire damage on entry-level plastics and the more advanced nanocomposites. The first example is a 1999 Hyundai Accent. The consumption of upholstery, seat foam, and dashboard is considerably greater than the consumption of polymerics and nanocomposites present on the 1999 Chevrolet S-10 pickup truck. Both vehicles suffered identical fire mechanisms. The positive wire in the steering column wiring loom which feeds the ignition switch melted and caught fire while both the vehicles were parked.

Figure 4.1

Figure 4.2

Figure 4.3

Figure 4.4

In some polymeric composites, there may be a conversion factor when the material is exposed to extreme heat. A conversion factor is where one material is converted into a hazardous material by the application of heat from the fire. An example of this is fluoroelastomer composites. When an fluoroelastomer is strongly heated it will convert to hydrogen fluoride. This is a highly corrosive and flammable gas which condenses in water to form hydrofluoric acid. Normally the fire department will extinguish the fire using water, thus creating this hazard.[11]

Nanocomposite technology creates a plastic which will resist thermal degradation and have relatively small amounts of volatile gasses released in the destruction of the molecular levels. Even as this material degrades, it will retain the ability to resist flaming combustion. This is not to state that a nanocomposite will not burn. Everything will burn if exposed to sufficient heat. Even things considered nonflammable such as steel and cement will burn if exposed to a hot enough fire.

The propagation of fire through the vehicle's interior should follow the physical laws regarding fire behavior. There should be a path of communication for the fire to move from area to area. However, there is a good deal of disagreement in the area of what is termed "drop-down fire." This refers to the dripping of liquid pools of flaming polymeric and nanocomposite. There is a school of theory bandied about by firefighters which states that the dripping pools of flaming plastic will land on other plastics below the area of ignition and create other fire areas. If the pools of drop down fire are dropping on a flammable material such as paper then there is a chance of fire spreading. If the dripping pools of flaming plastic drop down onto nanocomposites or other nonflammable polymerics, then the chance of creating additional fire spread is minimal.

Testing of burning nanocomposites and polymerics by the National Institute of Standards and Technology have produced results which reflect that very little BTU load potential is produced by drop-down fire. Use of the "drop-down theory" for being the cause of the spread of an interior fire of an automobile should be approached using the utmost caution.[29]

The latest data available for the BTU load potential available from burning nanocomposites and polymerics was performed by National Institute of Standards and Technology in cooperation with General Motors. The test results were published in August 1998 using selected components from a 1997 minivan. The parts were tested for BTU load potential using a calorimeter to measure the VOCs in the heat plume and a Bunsen burner to initiate ignition. Once ignition was started, the Bunsen burner was removed as a heat source then the measurements were taken. Table 4.1 is the result of that testing. Please note the low heat transfer potential of these plastics.

Table 4.1
Heat Release Rate of Selected Plastics[29]

Vehicle Part	Polymer Mass	Peak Heat Release Rate (kW)
Isolated battery	ca 1.3	21
Battery plus battery cover	ca. 2	53
Battery in heated box	ca 1.3	88
Air intake resonator	1.14	85
Headlamp assembly	1.7	23
Brake master cylinder	N/A	10
Wiper tray (driver side)	1.7	53
Wiper tray (passenger side)	1.7	58
Hood liner (driver side)	0.5	25
Hood liner (passenger side)	0.5	16
Rear wheelhouse liner	0.56	85
Fuel tank (empty >PP<)	8.48	500
Front passenger seat	8	540

In summary, the critical analysis path for confident diagnosis of the automotive fire requires the investigating engineer to develop analytical abilities on several different skill levels. The steps should always be followed in order. The final analysis should be a culmination and opinion based on a review and inspection of all the available evidence. A suggested procedure is as follows:

- **Define the automobile.** The areas to establish here are what types of materials are inherent in the construction of the vehicle being inspected. Is the subject vehicle an entry-level vehicle or a luxury vehicle? As a general rule, the newer and the higher trim level of construction, the greater percentage of nanocomposite materials will be used. The best way to gain experience in the materials used in construction of different makes and models of vehicles is to study the different vehicles at several wrecking yards. Remove some of the pieces and de-code the material. The materials examined along with the year, make, model, and trim level should be recorded in a log for future reference.
- **Define the point of ignition.** The investigating engineer will need to establish the area of the vehicle the fire started in to be able to define a primary failed part. This requires development of skill levels in interpreting burn patterns. Again, the best method to gain experience is

to visit wrecking yards and study the fire patterns on vehicles which caught fire.

As noted above, the only type of accidental operational mode fire which can originate from the passenger compartment is an electrical one. These are typically the least destructive. However, the investigating engineer should not discount the possibility of the wiring loom igniting a flammable liquid as it burns away from the firewall.

- **Define the heat release rate.** This area of analysis requires that the investigating engineer develop an ability to define the heat transfer temperature by the types of metals and composites consumed and the rate at which they were consumed. This is a most subjective analysis. Independent burn testing of different components should be performed and logged. The test parameters will establish the minimum BTU load required to cause "x" amount of consumption.

  For example, a Bunsen burner can be used to melt a steering column aluminum housing. The BTU release rate for the Bunsen burner can be defined with reasonable accuracy. The amount of time of exposure to the Bunsen burner can be measured to arrive at an approximation of the minimum BTUs required to cause similar destruction when comparing the test samples to the real fire components. If the heat release rate does not match up reasonably well with the type of fire, then incendiary fire causes should be explored. Any type of dynamic testing performed should construct the test protocols such that the test fixture will resemble operating conditions as closely as possible.

- **Define the primary failed system.** This part of the analysis lists the systems located in the area of ignition that are capable of starting flaming combustion. One of the major pitfalls of defining the primary failed part is determining with confidence whether or not the primary failed part is a victim of the fire or the cause. Sometimes the part that caught fire was caused to heat by a different part of its subsystem.

  For example, the armature bushings on a HVAC motor are causing excessive drag from age and high mileage. This will draw more current through the circuit from the fuse panel, the fan switch, the series resistor, the connectors, and the wire. The fan switch burns up and ignites. Here the part which caused the fire is the fan switch. The primary failed part was the HVAC blower motor.

One skill in particular which will be required is for the investigating engineer to be able to remove any suspected module and determine the current capability of that unit by the types of components mounted on the circuit board. Automotive computers which make decisions based upon memory and sensor input will not be equipped with the same large current-carrying busses and relays. Additionally, the wire size is generally larger. This skill level will require the ability to examine the burned remains of any automotive product and determine if that is an OEM unit or an aftermarket unit. If the primary failed part is non-OEM, then this dismisses any claims for warranty or subrogation against the manufacturer of the automobile. However, this does not preclude a finding of allowable subrogation against the manufacturer of the aftermarket part, installer, or repair shop.

Chapter 5

The Engineer in the Courtroom

Synopsis
5.1 Proper Investigation Techniques
5.2 Proper Scene Photography
5.3 Forensic Tools
5.4 Subrogation Issues
5.5 Arbitration
5.6 The Superior Court Action

5.1 Proper Investigation Techniques

When the claim for damage or defective product moves into the courtroom, the investigating engineer is subject to discovery by attorneys. Discovery is the legal process by which all information relevant to a particular case is reviewed and re-reviewed to arrive at the truth. This is where the skill level and method of reasoning employed by the investigating engineer is called to task by the attorney for the opposing side. If the person performing the investigation is not thoroughly qualified or the investigation is based on untested theory, their analysis and testimony may be excluded.

All investigation techniques should be patterned after the scientific method. The investigating engineer should avoid the trap of single-minded thinking. All evidence should be gathered and reviewed carefully before forming an opinion. Any sound opinion will arrive at the same hypothesis and conclusion using both inductive and deductive reasoning.

The seven steps to the scientific method are:

- **Recognize the need**. The need in this case is the fact that the automobile caught fire. There is either a warranty claim or an insurance claim creating the need to determine the primary failed part.
- **Define the problem**. The problem is that an analysis with confidence is required to establish any subrogation potential. The fact that there was a fire is already established. Next, any subrogation potential must be established.

- **Collect data.** All fire debris at the point of ignition needs to be sifted through to accumulate any remaining parts of components.
- **Analyze the data.** The fire debris must be analyzed using inductive reasoning to establish the heat release rate and the BTU load potential of the fire. The facts needed to be explored are whether or not the available fuel matches the evidence of BTU heat release.
- **Develop a hypothesis.** After the fire debris has been culled, the relevant particles have been analyzed, a point of ignition has been established, a BTU load potential has been defined, and a heat release rate approximation has been established, then a hypothesis for the primary failed part can be formed.
- **Test the hypothesis.** This will require procurement of an exemplar specimen of the suspected primary failed part. A test bench or test jig will need to be fabricated to operate the exemplar part. The test devised will need to be able to operate the exemplar part in a loaded and overloaded state. There is also the possibility that more than one test is required or there is more than one hypothesis to be tested.
- **Select the hypothesis.** The hypothesis which best fits the case facts and evidence established as fact should be selected as the prima facie case.

In conducting a proper investigation, the investigating engineer should review the fire department report, review any statements made by witnesses or the driver, and visit the site where the fire allegedly occurred. The drainage direction should be noted, the incline percentage should be measured and the burn pattern on the pavement should be analyzed if there was any flammable liquid spilling involved. No stone should be left unturned or else this will most likely be noted by one of the attorneys. If a pertinent fact was somehow missed by the investigating engineer, then this can throw doubt on the hypothesis for the primary failed part.

Essentially, the scientific method asks four questions: What do I know? How do I know that for a fact? Can my hypothesis be tested to support the conclusion? Can the results of the test be repeated with the same result? When the hypothesis formed supports examination by these questions, then this becomes what is defined as knowledge. If the engineer's hypothesis deviates from this procedure, any sharp attorney will realize this and attempt to have the hypothesis nullified as being "junk science."

When properly employed, the scientific method should work for both inductive reasoning and deductive reasoning. The facts should fit the hypothesis when working from a premise to a conclusion and working from a conclusion to a premise.

For example, an investigating engineer is assigned to determine if the fuel line installed six months ago by a local dealer ruptured and caused an engine fire. The investigation is started by examining the repair orders to verify what kind of work was performed. When the investigating engineer inspects the vehicle, the hood latch is damaged from the fire. The hood cannot be raised so the engine is inspected by looking at it from the underside. A hypothesis finding that there was a faulty fuel hose is formed without opening the hood. If an attorney finds this fact out, then the investigating engineer's opinion will be nullified because a thorough inspection was not performed. This report will be labeled as "junk science" because the scientific method was ignored.

Proper investigation technique requires a "hands-on" approach when applied to the analysis of fire. The investigating engineer will be called on to enumerate all the steps taken and the methodology used to form the expert opinion. Therefore, it is critical that the methods employed have the general support of the scientific community.

Complete disassembly of any affected area is required for access. The consumed areas must be carefully de-layered so that there is no destruction of evidence. Once evidence has been procured, it must be protected with a chain of custody protocol established to prevent any allegations of evidence spoilage.

To perform electrical system field analysis without the support of the correct workshop manual, the investigating engineer will need to develop skills in analyzing what function certain wires will perform based on size of wire in circuit, component location, and electronic board functioning. Essentially, the skill level will require that the person performing the de-layering and analysis be able to identify which circuit was affected and how it was affected by looking at the remains.

Many states require that the person investigating a fire, regardless of type, must hold a private investigator license. If the investigating engineer is working as a consultant for the manufacturer or an insurance carrier without a required license, then care must be taken in writing the report such that the focus is on mechanical issues. The engineering report must diagnose only the automobile or truck. The issues of investigating the owner or driver of the vehicle for possible arson motives must be performed by a person licensed to do that type of work in that state. The manufacturer is usually free to send any employee deemed qualified to examine the vehicle. It is only when the person conducting the fire investigation offers their services to the general public will they run afoul of the state legal requirements.

Essentially, the purview of the investigating engineer is to establish that there was or was not an operational mode failure. If there is a finding that there was no accidental reason for the subject vehicle to catch fire, then any further investigation will require a private investigator or certified fire investigator to work with the investigating engineer. Obviously, if the investigating engineer is working for a manufacturer, then his or her duties are truncated when the issue of a warranty claim is eliminated.

5.2 Proper Scene Photography

The investigating engineer will require some specialized photographic equipment for properly recording a vehicle fire. It does not matter who manufactures the camera equipment, only that a minimum quality of "entry-level professional" equipment be purchased. The suggested list of equipment is as follows.

- A 35-mm single lens reflex (SLR) camera body with detachable lens capability. The unit selected should have auto and manual focus along with auto and manual F-stop features. A built-in light meter is also a helpful feature.
- A 50-mm lens, a macro lens, and a wide-angle lens are required. The macro lens should have focus range down to 1 inch field of view. The 50-mm lens is the closest lens there is to photograph the way a human eye sees the subject matter. The wide-angle lens merely allows for a more comprehensive view of a larger area.
- There are three flash units required. The pop-up flash built into the SLR camera body, a detachable handheld flash, and a speed flash unit. Sometimes a speed flash unit is called a "ring flash." These are highly specialized flash units for use with the macro lens. A speed flash unit can be used for ranges down to a few inches. The pop-up flash unit on the SLR camera body can be used for ranges of 3 feet to a maximum of 7 feet. The handheld unit can be used at closer ranges. However, the flash light beam must be aimed so that it "bounces" off another surface to reflect onto the subject matter. All of the flash units should be equipped with auto range functions.
- A 35-mm handheld electronic camera. The unit selected should have telephoto and macro capabilities down to an 18-inch depth of focus, built-in auto flash, auto focus, and panorama settings. These types of cameras are most useful in areas where the conventional 35-mm camera will not fit and in use for undercarriage shots. Sometimes the only way to garner evidence is to hold this camera into the hole you wish to photograph and snap several different angles.
- A good digital camera. Quality level should be "pro-sumer" (professional/consumer) at a minimum. The unit selected should have capability to change lenses. A built-in pop-up flash in addition to a mountable

flash unit is desirable. The flash unit may require a proprietary extension cable to enable remote operation of flash unit.

- A small portable digital camera. There are several on the market. They are about the size of a deck of cards. There are even water-resistant units available. These small cameras have excellent macro capabilities when evidence photography requires the investigator to stick their hand with the camera into a small area to take photographs.
- Smartphones. If all else fails, the still and video cameras built into most modern smart phones will work to document difficult-to-reach areas.
- A handheld video camera auxiliary lamp. These are inexpensive units which are available in 40–80-watt models. Some models come with a "hot shoe" fitting so that the video cam light can be mounted to the top of the 35-mm SLR camera. These lamps are useful when photographing down into a dark hole when the ambient light is quite bright. The lamp can also be placed down at the bottom of the dark hole to illuminate the component desired.
- A handheld video cam with auto lamp function, digital auto focus, and digital stabilization features. It is suggested that both a film tape and a digital camera be available. Both formats will be needed for a court action and for digital communication.

Digital cameras will suffice for most fire investigation work. Most field work will involve photographing the subject matter under adverse lighting conditions. Film will reproduce a true color based upon the available light source. A digital camera will reproduce an electronically designated version of the colors. Sometimes, use of an umbrella or other shade device can assist with producing a better photograph under adverse lighting conditions. Use the umbrella or other shade device to block the glare of the sun.

The mention of 35mm film is made because some attorney firms require that film be used exclusively. While "trick" photography is possible, it is considerably more difficult to manipulate a positive print from a negative 35 mm film. Digital photography lends itself to manipulation of the photograph subject using digital photograph editing software. The investigating engineer and the CFI should be equally familiar with both types of photography.

First, the subject vehicle must be identified. This is performed by photographing the subject vehicle, the VIN plate, and the mileage, if possible. Starting from the exterior, there should be eight photographic angles taken. One photograph angle lined up diagonally with each corner of the subject vehicle, one from the front, one from the rear, and one from each side. The VIN plate is usually located on the left "B" pillar, driver's door, the front firewall, or the left corner of the dashboard. Some of the "confidential" locations of hidden VIN numbers are under one of the wheelhouse splash guards, under the driver seat, under the passenger seat, under the rear seat, on top of a frame rail under the truck bed, behind the brake master cylinder booster, and behind the rear license plate.

If possible, two separate identifications of the VIN number should be photographed. Photo record of the mileage may not be possible due to destruction or a digital odometer. However, a photograph of the destroyed odometer should be taken as part of the documentation.

Most vehicles sold on the U.S. market after 1990 use a set of "pre-delivery inspection" (PDI) labels. These are very specialized stick-on labels which only come with the new vehicle. These labels are included with the manifest papers which accompany each new vehicle prior to sale. The labels are imprinted with the VIN number of the individual vehicle. The dealership technician performing the PDI will affix one label to each hinged panel, both quarter panels, and both bumper covers. Many times the PDI labels can be used for secondary identification of the VIN and to determine if the subject vehicle is equipped with all the original parts. These PDI labels are only available with the new car manifest. They are not produced for sale as a separate part. Notably, these are the only labels on a modern vehicle which do not have a part number. All other labels can be replaced with new labels.

Second, the area of ignition should be carefully documented before any disassembly is performed. If the fire is electrical in nature, check and photograph any evidence of heat at the fusible links, fuses, wires, and relay connections.

For example, the electrical window switch assembly fails and starts a fire. The fire may be limited to the left or right door panel but there might also be signs of heat at the electrical source for the window switch.

Third, as the de-layering process progresses, each removed component must be individually photographed from all angles. A suggestion here is that a large blue towel be used for a background to photograph the component against. A blue background will assist the film true color development. The blue background will absorb light and eliminate shadows on the subject matter better than a more reflective surface.

In summary, photographic evidence is the best type of evidence to gather. To assure the proper exposure, take several shots of the same subject matter from different angles. Given the difficult nature of photographing automobiles' crevices, it is best to take more exposures than just one. The flash unit can be held such that the light reflects from another surface rather than directly on the photographic subject. Experiment with differing angles, focus ranges, and flash settings to obtain optimal photographic evidence. The cost of using a few extra rolls of film or sorting through a number of digital photographs to "cherry pick" the good ones pales in comparison to the cost of paying an engineer to return to the subject vehicle to get a better photograph of the subject matter. Another factor to consider is that most insurance carriers desire to dispose of the burned automobile carcass as quickly as possible to avoid escalating storage fees.

5.3 Forensic Tools

Forensic tools in the automotive fire area are used primarily for the detection of fraud and arson. The investigating engineer should be familiar with all of the types of testing and methodologies.

Arson and fraud are difficult crimes to establish sufficient evidence for a criminal prosecution. Regardless of whether or not there is sufficient evidence is immaterial. All evidence must be examined and tested with equal and impartial expertise. It should be noted that a finding of incendiary automotive fire will likely result in the insurance carrier filing a report with an organization called the National Insurance Crime Bureau (NICB) or another database firm such as Independent System Operator (ISO).

The NICB is a massive database company which stores confidential reports from insurance carriers, tracks and cross-links claims information, conducts investigations, and assists with the prosecution of perpetrators. This is a private company which cannot be accessed by private individuals, private investigators, or non-insurance firms. Their business model focuses exclusively on insurance carriers.

The first tool discussed was the field service combustible gas analyzer or "sniffer." This tool can be effective only if the investigating engineer receives the assignment and is granted access in a very short period of days.

One of the major problems with using this tool is that it is somewhat unreliable. However, it can be used as an indicator so that evidence can be gathered for lab analysis.

If an accelerant is suspected, and the subject vehicle has been allowed to sit exposed to air, then the vast majority of any accelerant will have evaporated because the most common compounds are aromatic. The sooner the suspect sample material is sent to the lab, the better the chances are for a positive finding presence of an accelerant.

One confounding factor is that most automotive fire is extinguished using water by the local fire department. This has the effect of diluting any signs of remaining accelerant. Additionally, the fire department or tow truck driver has a propensity to sweep the pavement under the vehicle and dump the debris back into the vehicle. If the pavement is made of asphalt, the hydrocarbons found in asphalt mix may contaminate the evidence.

A second confounding factor occurs when the fuel tank ruptures and a quantity of flaming gasoline is present. The air entraining through the vehicle may carry VOC's from the gasoline formula and deposit them on the interior surfaces of the vehicle. Moreover, many vehicles have a fuel pump service hatch located under the rear seat. The purpose of this hatch is to allow servicing of the fuel pump assembly from the fuel tank without having to remove the fuel tank from the vehicle. If the hatch melts or dislodges, this can also allow for air entrainment to deposit components of gasoline into the vehicle. Either example will result in a suspect or contaminated GC/MS reading at the lab.

The next tool is one of the most important the investigating engineer has in their toolbox: the simulated test. To measure the results of whatever piece of material is being tested, it is necessary to accurately measure the heat produced. Thermometers, pyrometers, and thermocouples are the most commonly used.

A thermometer will measure heat up to around 250–1,000°F. Pyrometers will range from 500–3,000°F. Pyrometers typically come in "J"- and "K"-type probes. The J-type is for temperatures up to 1,500°F while the K-type probe is used for higher temperatures. Thermocouples range from 0–3,000°F.

One of the most common mistakes in creating a proper test is the failure of the engineer to adjust for line drop. When creating a test measurement protocol, use an adjustable thermo-probe which has the adjustment screw in the handle of the probe. All wire has some resistance. Even relatively small lengths of wire will cause digital measuring equipment to read inaccurately.

Proper calibration protocol requires that the test equipment be calibrated to allow for the natural resistance found in wire (line drop). This is achieved by immersing probe in ice water and adjusting the meter to 32°F. Any signal loss from line drop resistance will then be compensated for.

Another popular tool to use is an infrared non-contact thermometer-pyrometer. These tools are available in different heat range measurements up to 3,500°F.

An infrared thermometer works by measuring the reflected energy, transmitted energy, and the emitted energy from the surface of the material being measured. The input reading is interpreted and averaged by an internal processor. The approximate reading of the surface temperature being measured will display on the unit digitally.

Emissivity is the measure of the ability of the surface being tested to emit infrared energy. Most organic materials and painted surfaces are good emitters with an emissivity of approximately 95 percent. The owner's manual for the infrared unit selected will indicate if the unit has been calibrated for the natural 5-percent loss in emissivity. Many units are precalibrated for natural loss. If not, be sure to take this into consideration when making final temperature readings.

Shiny or polished metals have a low emissivity rate. To measure the emissivity of shiny or polished metals it is necessary to apply tape, flat black paint, or a suitable spray coating which will not be consumed by the test heat.

Table 5.1 contains the emissivity rate for common automotive materials. The values are approximate.

Both steel and iron are somewhat poor emitters of infrared energy. An adjustment in the temperature readings will have to be made when measuring the infrared heat of an engine or exhaust manifold. The calculations will have to be prepared with caution as the true value of the reading may be as much as 30 percent off from the read out value on the infrared meter.

To obtain exact surface temperature use a K-type surface probe for a pyrometer to get an exact reading on the exemplar exhaust manifold then compare this reading with one taken with the infrared meter. Several such comparisons provide a good indication of the infrared meter's accuracy. This testing will provide validation of calculated emissivity values.

Table 5.1
Table of Common Emissivities

Aluminum, oxidized	0.30
Asbestos and organic brake pads	0.95
Asphalt	0.95
Basalt	0.70
Brass	0.50
Carbon	0.85
Ceramic	0.95
Concrete	0.95
Copper, Oxidized	0.95
Dirt	0.94
Glass	0.85
Ice	0.98
Iron, Oxidized	0.70
Lead	0.50
Oil	0.94
Paint	0.93
Plastics, opaque over 20-mm thick	0.95
Rubber	0.95
Sand	0.90
Snow	0.90
Steel, Oxidized	0.80
Textiles	0.94
Water	0.93

The next tool which the investigating engineer has is a process called gas chromatography. The gas chromatograph unit is used in conjunction with a PC to allow visual display of results and a printout. The sample is volatilized in the injection port of the gas chromatograph and is pushed by a known gas such as helium or nitrogen into and through the gas column. The column is the heart of the gas chromatograph since this is where the components of the flammable liquid are separated.[18]

The critical analysis path here for the investigating engineer is to establish that there was an accelerant present in the passenger area which was not cargo being lawfully carried or having splashed in the area somehow.

Another area for the engineer to consider is that when an accelerant is used on the interior of an automobile, the whole interior is usually destroyed. The investigating engineer may reason with confidence that any trace of an accelerant could not possibly have survived the inferno. Such reasoning is sound in the majority of cases. However, samples must be gathered and processed by a fire evidence lab anyway. If the investigating engineer fails to perform the gas chromatograph test, then an argument may be made that an incomplete investigation was made.

When considering the sample to send to the lab, it is best to send as porous a sample as is available. The accelerant will have evaporated or been consumed from any smooth surface. As noted above, the sample should be gathered as soon as possible after the fire.

The third forensic tool the investigating engineer has is the process of spectrochemical analysis of on-board fluids. This process will typically test oil, transmission oil, power steering fluid, brake fluid, and coolant.

This test is used to determine if the subject vehicle has a major component beginning to fail or that has already failed. The accuracy of this process has been proven over years of accepted use by the heavy truck industry and scientific community. The tests are conducted in compliance with ASTM Codes and Standards for fluid analysis.

If it can be shown that the subject vehicle has a blown engine or transmission, then this establishes a financial motive for the owner of the vehicle to deliberately set the vehicle ablaze to collect the insurance.

For example, a vehicle fire has been determined to be suspicious in origin. An engine oil sample is gathered and sent to the lab for analysis. The spectrochemical analysis sheet shows that there is both a fuel contamination problem along with abnormal levels of only tin, copper and lead. No other wear metals are present in abnormal levels.

From this reading it can be established that the engine has had an ongoing problem with fuel dilution in the oil for many thousands of miles prior to the date of loss. This is evidenced by the fact that the vast majority of engine bearings are made up of several material overlays. The most common design is a Tri-metal bearing. The back part of the bearing shell is comprised of aluminum. On top of the backing, there are usually six to eight layers of a material called "babbitt." The main ingredients of this material are tin, copper and lead. On top of the babbitt layers are six to eight layers of aluminum. This layer of aluminum is precisely polished to the exact dimension of the bearing specifications.

If the spectrochemical analysis test reveals abnormal or critical levels of tin, copper, and lead, but no aluminum, then it can be deduced that the top layers of aluminum were flushed out of the engine from prior oil changes. The fuel dilution was caused by a faulty engine management component. This compromised the ability of the oil to lubricate. This in turn caused the accelerated wear of the bearings. Therefore, the engine has had a bearing deterioration problem dating back prior to the date of the fire.

The critical analysis path for the investigating engineer to understand from the spectrochemical analysis test is that this test will detect only wear metal particles which are small enough to suspend themselves into the oil. If the particles are gravimetrically heavier than the oil, the particles will fall out of suspension. Thus, the test will only detect wear metals. Catastrophic destruction chunks will not be rated by this test. This establishes the reliability of the spectrochemical test to test for wear metals along with lubricity, and fluid contaminants.

5.4 Subrogation Issues

Subrogation is the legal process whereby third party liability is established. Part of the assignment the investigating engineer will receive is to determine if there exists any viable subrogation issues.

The legal arena of subrogation is actually quite large. It encompasses personal injury, property damage, loss of use of home, vehicle or both, and business interruption. The focus of the automotive fire subrogation issue is on property damage.

If the investigating engineer is working for a manufacturer and there is a claim for warranty damage due to component failure, then the focus of the investigation with regard to subrogation is to establish who manufactured the component that failed. If the component that failed and caused the fire is supplied by a sub-vendor, then all or part of the damage loss should be paid by that sub-vendor or their product liability insurance carrier.

Another area of subrogation which should be explored is whether or not recent vehicle repair work caused the failure and resultant fire damage. For example, the power steering hose was recently replaced by a repair shop. The hose leaked while under warranty and caught the engine on fire. The two issues to separate here are whether or not the hose failed due to a defect in the labor or the material.

Primarily, the subrogation issues in analyzing automotive fire relate to a defective component under factory warranty, a defect in labor from recent repair work, a defect in parts from recent repair work, deliberate vandalism where perpetrator is known, or aftermarket optional equipment installed.

The critical path for the investigating engineer to understand here is that it is not incumbent upon the engineer to have the skills of a subrogation attorney. However, some skills in recognizing subrogation potential should be developed so that the manufacturer or insurance carrier can be properly advised. It is incumbent upon the investigating engineer to be able to establish with certainty the hypothesis or theory of failure so that the subrogation process will have a successful outcome.

5.5 Arbitration

Arbitration is a legal process whereby claims are mediated. Most insurance carriers will have a clause in the policy that non-binding arbitration is required of the insured before legal action can be initiated. Many insurance policies are written with a binding arbitration clause. Many insurance carriers belong to and adhere to the rules of an "arbitration forum." This process is much like agreed binding arbitration between insurance carriers. The purpose is to settle liability issues without having to engage in a protracted court battle.

Arbitration will be the first stage where the expertise of the investigating engineer will be called to task. This examination of the expert witness is a legal process called "voir dire." The purpose of this procedure is to determine if the investigating engineer has the sufficient skill level to be considered an expert witness.

As a general rule, the rules of evidence and procedure are somewhat relaxed in the arbitration process. The process is typically conducted by either a retired judge or attorney who is familiar with the disposition and resolution of similar cases in the jurisdiction.

The arbitration process usually takes place in the office of the arbitrator. The arbitrator is a neutral third party who will hear the evidence from both parties. Based on the evidence and the testimony of the expert witnesses, the arbitrator makes a decision as to who is the responsible party and how much should be paid in damages.

The critical analysis path here is for the investigating engineer to be able to demonstrate by means of education, knowledge, skill, experience, or specialized training that this person possesses expertise in the area of automobile fire. This is best achieved by having solid skill levels in automotive materials, mechanisms for fire, experience in field service, knowledge of the manufacturing process, knowledge of repair procedures, knowledge of the usual and customary practices in both dealer operations and auto repair shops, industry standards, test procedures and specialized training in subrogation.

In a nutshell, this is the primary reason why the interpretation of fire evidence will vary so drastically between fire investigators and engineers. A fire investigator who has never worked a day in his or her life in the automobile industry will not have the same understanding of automobiles, and their construction, or of troubleshooting a problem as will an engineer who has spent a lifetime working for automobile manufacturers. Additionally, if the investigating engineer has not had sufficient cross-training from his or her employment, then that person may not be the best candidate for expert analysis. Experience and manufacturer training is what counts in the automotive world. Proprietary technology is not taught in public university.

5.6 The Superior Court Action

In a Superior Court action, the investigating engineer is called on to act in the capacity as an expert witness. An expert witness in the U.S. judicial system is a person who assists the trier of fact. This person will assist the court in the interpretation of evidence by reducing the technical issues into language which the average juror will be able to understand. The role of the expert witness is to render expert opinion in an non-prejudicial manner.

The expert witness is the most powerful technical resource in the presentation of any significant automotive lawsuit. Because of well-publicized verdicts and the societal trend toward a risk-free environment, litigation consulting has become big business for many automotive engineering experts and related professionals. With millions often at stake, not surprisingly, there has been some evolutionary blurring of the distinction between an attorney who is ethically bound to provide zealous representation in an advocacy setting and an expert witness who traditionally provided neutral and detached testimony on complicated technical or scientific issues. Through the years, judges in various jurisdictions applied decreasing amounts of threshold screening for the admissibility of expert testimony.

Until the 1990s, existing law in federal courts was governed by *Frye v. United States*, a 1923 decision which stated that expert opinion based on a scientific technique is inadmissible unless that technique is "generally accepted" as reliable in the relevant scientific community. Further, expert opinion based on methodology that diverges "significantly from the procedures accepted by recognized authorities in the field" cannot be shown to be generally accepted as reliable technique.[15]

Consider this rationale for a moment. In the 1920s the United States had barely emerged from World War I. As a society, the airplane was still in its infancy, cars went barely 50 mph, medical procedures were scarcely different than those performed 100 years prior, and most houses didn't have a refrigerator or a city sewer line. In terms of modern science, society was still fairly primitive. Our understanding of science was limited, yet the "prove it to me with approved scientific methods" mentality was the core of judicial decision.

Under the Federal Rules of Evidence relevant evidence is admissible. Relevant evidence is evidence having any tendency to make the existence of any fact that is of consequence to the determination of the lawsuit more or less probable than it would be without the evidence.

In federal court and many state courts, testimony of experts is governed by the following Federal Rules of Evidence:[14]

> **Rule 702. Testimony of Experts**. If scientific, technical, or other specialized knowledge will assist the trier of fact to understand the evidence or to determine a fact in issue, a witness qualified as an expert by knowledge, skill, experience, training, or education, may testify thereto in the form of an opinion or otherwise.
>
> **Rule 703. Bases of Opinion Testimony by Experts**. The facts or data in the particular case upon which an expert bases an opinion or inference may be those perceived by or made known to the expert at or before the hearing. If of a type reasonably relied upon by experts in the particular field in forming opinions or inferences upon the subject, the facts or data need not be admissible in evidence. These rules grant expert witnesses testimonial latitude unavailable to regular witnesses because an expert's opinion is presumed to have reliable basis in the knowledge and experience of the relevant discipline.

Before the introduction of the statutory federal evidence rules, the admissibility of expert testimony was governed by *Frye v. United States*. This brief 1923 District of Columbia Court of Appeals decision affirmed the murder conviction of James Frye. As part of his defense, Mr. Frye attempted to introduce the results of a deception test performed on him. This deception test was a crude precursor to the lie detector test. The accused's expert claimed scientific experimentation demonstrated that various emotions, including conscious deception, raised the systolic blood pressure. After the prosecution's objection, the trial court excluded this evidence as well as the accused's offer to have this deception test repeated in front of the jury.

In upholding the conviction, the Court of Appeals in *Frye* noted that the point where a scientific principle crosses the line between the experimental and accepted stages is somewhat difficult to define. Somewhere in this "twilight zone," the scientific principle must be recognized. Noting that courts will admit expert testimony deduced from well-recognized scientific principle, the deduction must be sufficiently established to gain the "general acceptance" in the particular field in which it belongs. In *Frye*, the Court of Appeals held that the systolic blood pressure deception test had not yet gained standing and scientific recognition in the psychological community.

The *Frye* decision's "general acceptance" test became the yardstick by which courts traditionally evaluated the admissibility of scientific testimony.

The next relevant case which established the admissibility of expert witness testimony was *Daubert v. Merrell Dow Pharmaceuticals, Inc*. This defined the role of the original trial judge as the evidentiary "gatekeeper."

Jason Daubert and Eric Schuller were children born with serious birth defects. During pregnancy, their mothers had been prescribed Bendectin, an anti-nausea drug marketed by Merrell Dow Pharmaceuticals. They sued Merrell Dow, alleging Bendectin caused the birth defects. After extensive discovery, Merrell Dow filed a motion for summary judgment asking the court to dismiss the case contending that Bendectin does not cause birth defects in humans and that the plaintiffs had no competent evidence to show that it does. Merrell Dow supported its motion with the affidavit of Dr. Steven Lamm, a well-credentialed physician and epidemiologist, on the risk of exposure to various chemical substances. Dr. Lamm stated that he had reviewed all of the literature on Bendectin, including more than 30 published studies involving 130,000 patients. Dr. Lamm concluded that the use of Bendectin by expectant mothers was not a demonstrated risk factor for birth defects in humans.

In opposing Merrell Dow's summary judgment motion, plaintiffs presented the testimony of eight similarly credentialed experts who concluded that Bendectin can cause birth defects. Rather than human subjects, however, these conclusions were based on test tube and animal studies that linked Bendectin and malformations. The plaintiffs' experts' conclusions were also based on studies of the chemical structure of Bendectin that showed similarities between it and another substance known to cause birth defects. Additionally, these conclusions were based on a reanalysis of previously published human statistical studies.

The trial court granted Merrell Dow's motion after it concluded that plaintiffs' scientific evidence did not have general acceptance in its field. Because there was a vast body of human epidemiological data concerning Bendectin, the court ruled that an expert opinion not based on this epidemiological evidence was inadmissible to establish causation. The Ninth Circuit Court of Appeals upheld this decision ruling that expert opinion based on scientific test technique is inadmissible unless that technique is "generally accepted" as reliable in the relevant scientific community. Expert opinion based on methodology that diverges significantly from the procedures accepted by recognized authorities in the field cannot be shown to be "generally accepted" as reliable technique. In its ruling, the Ninth Circuit Court of Appeals characterized plaintiffs' statistical reanalysis as "unpublished, not subjected to the normal peer review process, and generated solely for use in litigation."

The plaintiffs appealed to the U.S. Supreme Court. In its landmark 1993 *Daubert* decision, the U.S. Supreme Court vacated the lower court's rulings. In doing so, the U.S. Supreme Court ruled that the "general acceptance" standard outlined in *Frye* is not an essential condition for the admissibility of scientific evidence. The court noted that Federal Rule of Evidence 702 assigns federal judges the task of ensuring that expert testimony rests on a reliable foundation and is relevant. Pertinent evidence based on scientifically valid principles satisfies these requirements.

In so ruling, the U.S. Supreme Court noted that there are important differences between the quest for truth in the courtroom and the quest for truth in the laboratory. Science is advanced by broad consideration of a multitude of hypotheses. Those that are incorrect are eventually shown to be so. However, conjectures that are probably wrong are of little use in achieving the judicial system's goal of a quick, final and binding legal judgment about a particular set of events occurring in the past.

The U.S. Supreme Court acknowledged that the "gatekeeper" role given to federal judges, no matter how flexible, will inevitably prevent a jury, on occasion, from learning authentic insights and innovations. Nevertheless, this is the balance struck by federal evidence rules which were not designed for the "exhaustive search for cosmic understanding, but for the particularized resolution of legal disputes" (*General Electric v. Joiner*).

Sifting through the *Daubert* rhetoric, the "gatekeeper" function assigned to federal judges requires them to make a preliminary assessment of whether the questioned expert's underlying reasoning or methodology is scientifically valid and can be properly applied to the facts at issue. The inquiry is a "flexible one," and its focus must be solely on the principles and methodologies, not on the conclusions that they generate.

The *Daubert* test for admissibility of questioned scientific evidence bears on four crucial factors:

- **testing**. Whether the theory or technique in question can be and has been tested.
- **peer review**. Whether the theory or technique has been subjected to peer review and publication.

- **error rate and standards**. What is the known or potential error rate in the theory and are there existing standards controlling the technique's operation.
- **widespread acceptance**. Whether the theory has attracted widespread acceptance within the relevant scientific community.

Thus, the *Frye* test and the *Daubert* test became the deciding factors as to whether or not the expert's testimony would be heard by the jury. The *Daubert* decision firmly established the role of the trial judge as the "gatekeeper" of the evidence which would be heard by the court. A point to note here is that the *Daubert* test applied only to scientific evidence and not other disciplines.[8]

The role of the trial judge was expanded by the U.S. Supreme Court decision in the case of *General Electric v. Joiner*. In this decision, the court responded to allegations that decisions following *Daubert* were too restrictive.

In the 1997 *General Electric* decision, a city electrician contracted lung cancer and sued the manufacturer of polychlorinated biphenyls (PCBs), the manufacturers of electric transformers, and the manufacturers of dielectric fluids. The trial court excluded the testimony of the electrician's experts and granted summary judgment. The Eleventh Circuit Court of Appeals overturned the trial court's decision. On appeal, the U.S. Supreme Court ruled that the trial court did not abuse its discretion either in excluding the scientific opinions offered by the electrician's experts indicating that infant mice developed cancer after receiving massive doses of PCBs or in excluding expert opinions based on epidemiological studies.

The trial court had concluded that the animal studies on which the electrician's experts relied did not support the opinion that exposure to PCBs had contributed to his cancer. These studies involved infant mice that had developed cancer after being exposed to massive doses of PCBs injected directly into their abdominal organs in a highly concentrated form. The fluid to which the electrician had been exposed had a much smaller concentration of PCBs. The cancer found in test mice was different than that contracted by the electrician. Finally, one of the electrician's experts admitted that no study had demonstrated that PCBs lead to cancer in any other species.

Thus, in the *General Electric* decision the role of "evidentiary gatekeeper" was more broadly defined and given latitude at the trial judge level.[16]

The role of the expert was expanded in a 1998 case, *Pillow v. General Motors*. Judy Pillow sued General Motors, alleging that the brake system on her 1988 Chevrolet van was defectively designed after she rear ended a pickup truck and was injured. Specifically, she alleged that the master cylinder and brake pedal components were violently thrust rearward toward the driver's right foot in this frontal impact. Ms. Pillow's expert witness was prepared to testify that:

- the forces on the brake system of plaintiff's van were transmitted through the brake pedal causing plaintiff's ankle injuries;
- the design of the brake master cylinder and related components was defective and unreasonably dangerous; and
- the brake system should have been designed so that the master cylinder was positioned sideways or at an angle such that forces would not be transmitted to the brake pedal.

General Motors moved to exclude the testimony of plaintiff's expert under the *Daubert* decision guidelines.

In analyzing the *Daubert* factors, the court noted that the expert did not conduct an independent crash test. Rather, he relied on a barrier crash test which depicted a crash configuration that differed in speed, angle, and type of impact. Further, the expert had not tested his alternative design theory nor did he demonstrate that it complied with the appropriate safety standards. On this issue, the court concluded that the testimony consisted of "entirely untested opinions."

Secondly, the court examined the issue of peer review noting that scrutiny of the scientific community is a component of "good science" because it increases the likelihood that substantive flaws and methodology will be detected. In this case, the court noted that plaintiff had not established that her expert's theories had been subjected to any form of meaningful and favorable peer review.

In considering the third and fourth *Daubert* factors, the court noted that since the expert had not conducted any testing, there could not be a known rate of error. Additionally, plaintiff had not offered any evidence regarding the general acceptance in the scientific community of her expert's theories. For these reasons, the trial court excluded the plaintiff's expert.[19,31]

There was one interesting aspect of the *Pillow* decision: the trial court ruled in 1998 that *Daubert* applied not only to scientific evidence but also to technical or other specialized expert testimony from engineers.[19]

In a recent Tenth Circuit Appeals Court decision, *Truck Insurance v. Magne-Tek, Inc.*,[36] the *Daubert* standards were applied to a fire expert's testimony on the subject of pyrolysis which resulted in the exclusion of that testimony.

The underlying case was a subrogation action from a fire loss. Truck Insurance was the insurance carrier for a Colorado restaurant. The local fire department investigators and a private fire cause and origin investigator both formed the opinion that the fire started in a ceiling-floor void. The only heat source located near the point of ignition was a fluorescent light fixture. The fluorescent lamp ballast was the suspected cause.

Testing revealed that the overheat safety cutout switch inside the ballast was still functioning normally. It would have cut the electricity to the ballast if internal temperature reached 340°F.

The plaintiff's expert (a physicist) opined that pyrolysis must have occurred over a period of years which led to the lower ignition temperature from the formation of pyrophoric carbon.

Essentially, the court ruled that wood pyrolysis cannot be considered as a viable fire theory. The evidence used by the fire expert was judged to be inadmissible under *Daubert* because the evidence was not based on a scientific study even though pyrolysis testimony has been used and accepted as a fire theory in both state and federal courts for over 30 years. The only evidence presented by the expert in support of his position were three published articles. However, the court ruled that all three articles did not scientifically support the position of the expert. Rather, the articles cast doubt on the methodology used and were not supported by general consensus in the scientific community.

This does not affirm that the pyrolysis phenomena does not occur. Rather, the case holds that there is currently insufficient scientific testing performed to support a legal conclusion that it does occur.

In conclusion, the investigating engineer may be called on to testify in a Superior Court action. The opposing side will most certainly subject the engineer to the tests set forth in the cases cited above before his or her testimony will be allowed as an expert witness. Knowledge of the concepts required of the role of an expert witness will assist the investigating engineer from making mistakes which will ultimately result in the limitation or exclusion of his or her testimony. If at all possible, the expert witness should devise a test to illustrate the theory. A successfully tested theory will be much more compelling evidence than untested conjecture.

For the investigating engineer to testify successfully in a fire case, it requires a solid understanding of the following:

- automotive design and materials.
- fire mechanisms relating to individual systems.
- fire behavior given the compartmentalized configuration of vehicles.
- technical operation and specifications of the component in question.
- ability to demonstrate the known BTU load and heat release factors of materials or flammable or combustible liquids.
- knowledge of automotive polymerics and nanocomposites.
- electrical and electronic systems.
- applicable ISO, SAE, and ASTM standards.

This specialized knowledge and skill level are essential to reducing what can be a very technical subject down into layman terms so that the jury does not become confused.

References

1. American Society of Testing and Materials. *Standard Number D-1600-Standard Terminology Relating to Abbreviations, Acronyms, and Codes for Terms Relating to Plastics* (West Conshohocken, PA: ASTM International Publishing, 1999).

2. Theodore Baumeister, Eugene A. Avallone and Theodore Baumeister III. *Mark's Standard Handbook for Mechanical Engineers*, 5th ed. (Warrendale, PA: Society of Automotive Engineers Publishing, 2001).

3. *Black's Law Dictionary*, 7th ed. (St. Paul, MN: West Group Publishers, 1999).

4. Bosch Technical Publications. *Motronic Engine Management*, D-70442 (Stuttgart: Robert Bosch GmbH, 1994).

5. Bosch Technical Publications. *Bosch Automotive Engineers Handbook*, D-70442 (Stuttgart: Robert Bosch GmbH, 2000).

6. *CASTI Metals Black Book, North American Ferrous Data*, 4th ed. (Alberta: Canada, CASTI Publishing, Inc., 2002).

7. Lee Cole. *Investigation of Motor Vehicle Fires*, 4th ed. (San Anselmo, CA: Lee Books, 2001).

8. *Daubert v. Merrell Dow Pharmaceuticals, Inc.,* 509 U.S. Supreme Court, 579, 1993.

9. John D. DeHahn. *Kirk's Fire Investigation Techniques*, 5th ed. (Upper Saddle River, NJ: Prentice-Hall, 2002).

10. Deutsche Institut für Normung (DIN). *Standard Number 72552: Marking of Electronic Terminals; Standard Number 260: Marking of Polymeric Materials.* (Germany: DIN Publishers).

11. Mack Dreyer. *Technical Publication Information Paper Number 6* (Queensland Government Publishing, 1997).

12. James E. Duffy. *Auto Electricity and Electronics* (South Holland, IL: Goodheart-Wilcox, 1995).

13. Federal Code of Regulations, Title 49, Chapter 5, Section 571, Sub-Sections 106: Brake Fluid Hose Composition; 116: Brake Fluid; 301: Fuel System Integrity; 302: Interior Flammability (Washington, DC: U.S. Government Printing Office).

14. Federal Rules of Evidence, United States Code Sections: 702: Testimony of Experts; 703: Bases of Opinion Testimony by Experts (Washington, DC: U.S. Government Printing Office).

15. *Frye v. United States, District of Columbia,* Court of Appeals, 293 F., 1013, 1923.

16. *General Electric v. Joiner,* 522 U.S. Supreme Court, 136, 1997.

17. Don Goodsell. *Dictionary of Automotive Engineering*, 2nd ed. (Oxford, England: Butterworth-Heinemenn, Linacre House, 2002).

18. Dennis A. Guenther, Larry G. Goodwin and Ronald N. Thaman. *Forensic Analysis of Automobile Fires*, Society of Automotive Engineers Technical Paper Number 810011 (Warrendale, PA: Society of Automotive Engineers, 1981).

19. Frank Hostetler. *Expert Testimony*, SAE Accident Reconstruction TOPTEC Conference December 9-10, 1999 (SAE Continuing Professional Development Publishing, 1999).

20. Darrel A. Hilago. *Flammability Handbook for Plastics* (NY: Norstrand Rheinhold, 2000).

21. International Standards Organization (ISO). Standards Numbers 470 and 1087: Terminology and Vocabulary of Plastics; 1043-1: Basic Polymers and Their Special Characteristics; 1043-2: Fillers and Reinforcing Materials; 1043-4: Fire Retardants; 1629: Rubber and Lattices; 11469: Generic Identification and Marking of Plastic Materials; 14004: Marking and Designation of Recyclable Parts, (Geneva: ISO Publishing, reproduced by Global Engineering Documents).

22. American Isuzu. *Isuzu Trucks Body Building Guide* (Whittier, CA: Isuzu Technical Publications, 1999).

23. Land Rover of North America. Technical Publication Series: *Pre-Delivery Inspection* (Lanham, MD: Land Rover Publishing, 1999).

24. Land Rover of North America. Technical Publication Series: *Basic Electrical* (Lanham, MD: Land Rover Publishing, 1999).

25. Alpha Wire Company. Technical Publication Series (Lidgerwood, New Jersey, 2004).

26. National Fire Protection Association. Special Publication Number 51, *Flash Point Index of Trade Name Liquids* (Quincy, MA: NFPA Publishing, 2000).

27. National Fire Protection Association. Publication Number 921, *Guide for Fire and Explosion Investigations* (Quincy, MA: NFPA Publishing, 2002).

28. G.H.F. Nayler. *Dictionary of Mechanical Engineering*, 4th ed. (Warrendale, PA: Society of Automotive Engineering, 2002).

29. Thomas J. Ohlemiller and John R. Shields. *Burning Behavior of Selected Automotive Parts from a Minivan*, National Institute of Standards and Technology Research Paper Number 6143 (Gaithersburg, MD: NIST Publishing, 1998).

30. Keith Owen and Trevor Cooley. *Automotive Fuels Reference Guide*, 2nd ed. (Warrendale, PA: Society of Automotive Engineering, 1995).

31. *Pillow v. General Motors Corp,* 184 Federal Reporting District, US Supreme Court 304, East District Missouri Court, 1998.

32. *SAE Fuels and Lubricants Guide*, Technical Publication HS-23 (Warrendale, PA: Society of Automotive Engineering, 2000).

33. *SAE Handbook of Automotive Plastics* (Warrendale, PA: Society of Automotive Engineering, 2002).

34. Society of Automotive Engineering. Technical Standard Number J369—Interior Flammability of Composite Plastics; J1103—Composition and Characteristics of Brake Fluid; J1344-Marking of Plastic Parts, J1969—On-Board Diagnostics Program I; J1972—On Board Diagnostics Program II. In *SAE Handbook* (Warrendale, PA: Society of Automotive Engineering, 2003).

35. State of California Smog Check II Program. *Diagnostic and Repair Manual*, Department of Consumer Affairs Publication 1187 (Sacramento, CA: State Printing Office, 2001).

36. *Truck Insurance Exchange v. MagneTek, Inc.*, 10th Circuit Federal Appellate Court, February 25, 2004, Case No. WL348936.

37. Unocal Greases and Oils Division, Unocal Technical Publications Number 82 (Carson, CA: Unocal Corp Publishing).

38. Joseph D. Walters. *The Tire as a Vehicle Component*, SAE Publication Number C0101 (Warrendale, PA: Society of Automotive Engineering, 2002).

39. Martin Silberberg. *Chemistry: The Molecular Nature of Matter and Change, Fourth Edition.* (New York: McGraw-Hill Education, 2006).

40. P. B. Balbuena and Y. X. Wang (eds.). *Lithium Ion Batteries: Solid Electrolyte Interphase.* (London: Imperial College Press), 2004.

41. Gold Peak Industries Ltd. *Lithium Ion Technical Handbook.* 2000. Available at: www.gpina.com/pdf/Li-ion_Handbook.pdf.

42. U.S. Patent Number 4304825, United States Patent Office, DC, Maryland. Granted December 08, 1981.

About the Author

Gregory J. Barnett, AE, ASE, CFEI, CVFI has a career spanning over three decades as a technician, service engineer, field engineer, and automotive technology instructor. His experience is in both manufacturing and retail automotive.

Currently, he operates a field engineering and expert witness service offering hands-on engineering level diagnosis on automotive and heavy truck claims for major insurance carriers and attorneys.

Index

A

accelerant, 5, 9-10, 29, 41, 82-83, 101, 104, 106-109, 136-137, 151, 154

accident, 3, 5, 10, 12, 16, 42-43, 81, 84, 88, 98, 102, 106-109, 143, 147

alternator, 52, 55, 58, 61, 63-67, 86, 91, 100-101, 108, 113, 130

ambient, 5-6, 30-32, 35, 51, 111, 130, 149

ampacity, 5, 10, 90-91

ampere, 5, 7

arbitration, 156

arc, 5-6, 52, 61, 93-94, 96, 116

arc beading, 5-6, 93, 116

area of origin, 6, 61, 98, 125

arson, 3-4, 6-7, 102, 105, 147, 151

ASTM (American Society of Testing and Materials), 22-23, 25-26, 42, 100, 154, 163

autoignition, 6

AWG (American Wire Gauge), 57, 59-60, 87, 90-91

B

battery, 6, 52, 57-61, 63-68, 72, 74, 85-87, 90-93, 95-96, 104, 113, 115-123, 125-127, 130-133, 142

BLEVE (boiling liquid expanding vapor explosion), 6, 101

brake fluid, 37, 46, 74, 84, 154

BTU (British thermal unit), 4, 6, 8-9, 20, 39, 41, 45-46, 53, 61, 84, 97, 99, 109, 137, 141, 143, 146, 163

burn pattern, 29, 42, 83, 87, 98-99, 102, 106, 108-109, 136-137, 146

C

calorie, 6, 9

calorimeter, 6, 141

carrier, 1, 3, 6, 102, 109, 147, 151, 155-156, 162

catalytic converter, 30-32, 34-35, 39, 111, 130

code, 2, 4, 6-7, 14-16, 18-20, 22-23, 25, 30, 44, 69, 71, 109, 111, 123, 135

combustible, 6-9, 11, 28-29, 37, 39-41, 45, 53, 69, 72, 82, 93, 96-98, 102, 104, 136, 151, 163

combustible gas indicator, 7

conduction, 7, 108

convection, 7, 93, 108

coolant, 37, 39, 46-48, 63, 99, 107, 154

cross-sectional area, 57, 59

current, 5-7, 10, 54-57, 59-61, 63-65, 67-69, 71-72, 77, 83-84, 87, 90-91, 94, 104, 111-113, 119, 126-127, 132-133, 143